THE RACE BEFORE US

To Kim —

Thanks for all your
work on the manuscript.
With the author's
compliments & gratitude,

Bruce

THE RACE BEFORE US

A Journey of Running and Faith

Bruce H. Matson

Published by eChristian, Inc.
Escondido, California

Mission Books

The Race Before Us: A Journey of Running and Faith

Copyright © 2013 by Bruce H. Matson. All rights reserved.

First printing in 2013 by eChristian, Inc.
eChristian, Inc.
2235 Enterprise Street, Suite 140
Escondido, CA 92029
http://echristian.com

ISBN: 978-1-61843-348-0

Cover and interior design by Larry Taylor.

Project Staff: Dave Veerman, Linda Taylor, Ashley Taylor, Tom Shumaker, Tori Newhouse, and Sharon Wright.

Printed in the United States of America

19 18 17 16 15 14 13 12 8 7 6 5 4 3 2 1

Mission Books

*. . . let us run with perseverance the race
that is set before us.*

Hebrews 12:1 (NRSV)

CONTENTS

Foreword—"The Race" by Ravi Zacharias 9

Foreword—"The Run" by Frank Shorter 11

Acknowledgements 13

Introduction 15

Chapter 1—Hitting the Wall 19

Chapter 2—Hitting the Wall II 29

Chapter 3—Beginning to Run 39

Chapter 4—Beginning the Race (Philosophy 101) 47

Chapter 5—The Run: Making Progress (MTT) 65

Chapter 6—The Race: True for Me? 75

Chapter 7—The Run: Becoming a Runner 85

Chapter 8—The Race: A New Start 95

Chapter 9—Halfway (13.1 Miles) 109

Chapter 10—Colson's Proof: Running from Watergate 121

Chapter 11—The NYC Marathon 133

Chapter 12—Hitting the Wall—Again 149

Chapter 13—The Run: Beginning Again 153

Chapter 14—The Race: In Pursuit 169

Chapter 15—Participating in a Major 179

Chapter 16—Are We Kidding Ourselves? The God Delusion 189

Chapter 17—Winning the Race 201

Epilogue (Running with Ravi) 209

Bruce's Race Times 211

Eleven Commandments of Running 212

Top Ten Arguments for the Existence of the God of the Bible 213

Bibliography 215

Endnotes 219

Foreword—"The Race"

Too often we find out too late in life that attaining a pursuit and finding fulfillment are not necessarily the same thing. It is very possible to find meaning without extraordinary success, as the world deems success. Conversely, immense success does not always bring meaning or fulfillment with it.

As I travel the globe speaking and listening to so many voices, I am increasingly asked by business people for some insight into the meaning or purpose of life. After much success, many find a hunger that has not been met. Despite having achieved wealth, privilege, and professional recognition, these individuals are nagged by a deep, inner need yet unfulfilled. After four decades of covering every continent, I have witnessed that this sense of meaninglessness is a principal malady of the soul. I would go so far as to say that it has been the heart's deepest longing across generations and cultures. Solomon raised this subject centuries ago.

Whatever our experience, each of us must pause to ask ourselves if our paradigm of the world really matches reality. Is it coherent and is it livable—that is, consistent with one's worldview? Many are experiencing a profound emptiness because the success and accomplishments on which they had so intently focused cannot answer the four essential questions of life: How did life come to be? Why are we here? How do we determine right from wrong? What is our destiny?

From the first time I met Bruce, I sensed his deeply felt passion to make life count by living out the truth of life's essential purpose and wholeheartedly enjoying the relevance it brings. In *The Race Before Us*, Bruce confronts and unpacks this same pathos and these same questions. Using the Apostle Paul's wonderful metaphor of "the race," Bruce has captured the existential quest in his personal but engaging memoir of his own journey of faith. Bruce is a clear thinker and caring individual. As a lawyer, he wrestles with the obstacles to the Christian faith and seeks to know whether his answers do indeed match reality. *The Race* in one sense is every person's challenge. I am confident that anyone ready to embark on this race—in exploring why we are here, who God is, and how answers can be found in the person of Jesus Christ—will profit by going on this journey with Bruce. It is amazing how hours of serious thinking while training for the physical side of life has yielded the truth of ultimate fitness of body and soul. Every reader will benefit from Bruce's disciplines and gleanings.

—Ravi Zacharias
author and speaker

FOREWORD—"THE RUN"

Much to his good fortune, Bruce Matson discovered at age forty-nine that in some cases you can indeed "go home." For him this meant returning to the running of his youth. He completed a marathon when twenty-one and then proceeded to literally go off course for many years.

When I read Bruce's account of what happened after he finally confronted his own personal mortality, a wonderful French expression came to mind, *Plus ça change, plus il rest la même chose* (the more it changes, the more it stays the same). What follows is a very personal expression of an exceptional running journey back to spiritual, mental and physical health after staring into his own personal abyss.

Over the past forty years as running has become integrated into the lifestyles of many people around the world, more often than not those who stick with it do so because the activity becomes integrated into their daily lives and thoughts. Yes, it is a profound change that truly varies from person to person.

"More" does not adequately describe how Bruce evolved after he once again started putting one foot in front of the other. His is an intriguing story; particularly unusual in the way it involved huge, simultaneous changes in his ethics, morality, and view of religion. For some, like Bruce, running can do "much more" than simply help relieve stress.

For Bruce, in the twenty-eight years off-course, running was always there waiting for him to return. It was fun for me to be reminded that it is "the same" for many others out there as well.

—Frank Shorter

(1972 Olympic Gold Medal—marathon)

ACKNOWLEDGEMENTS

First and foremost, I am grateful to God for first running the race for me and then, with me. May this book be not for my recognition, but for His glory.

No one has shown me better how to be in the world while not being of the world more than my wife Cheryl. My tribute to her is throughout the book itself. For her remarkable patience, quiet example, and unwavering love, I am eternally grateful.

Many others helped along the way, of course—both in my running journey and my faith travels. At the risk of unintentionally forgetting someone, I am grateful to Jim Tonkowich, Caroline Coleman, Kerry Knott, Tom Tarrants, Gina Behrens, Art Lindsley, Mark Elliott, and Christine Coleman for their comments to various drafts (with a special thanks to our daughter Brooke, who was my best editor and critic); and to Dave Veerman for guiding me to eChristian and for his professional assistance with the manuscript.

I would never have made it around the streets of Richmond for more than a mile or two (I certainly would not have completed a single marathon) without the advice, guidance, and encouragement from Mike Hern, Dan Garber, Gene Rosen, Faith Hecht, Mary Damon, Val Siff, Gretchen Byrd, Andy Clark, Steve Romine, Ray King, Dewey Reynolds, Dan Blankenship, Sandy Lawson, and a number of YMCA 10K Training Team and Richmond Sports Backers' Marathon Training Team coaches whose names (I'm sorry) I cannot recall. Finally, I could never forget one person with whom I logged hundreds of miles around the streets of Richmond—a special thanks and much gratitude goes out to Dan Lynch, who will always be my running buddy.

This book, the journey it recounts, and the changed life that resulted would have never happened without the guidance, encouragement, persistence, and love (as well as, I know, considerable prayer) of my closest friend, Carl Meyer. This book would not have been written because I would have had no story to tell, except perhaps one of obesity, diabetes, and premature death and a life without a relationship with God. Since walking the campus together at William & Mary, Carl has shared books and tapes, engaged me in discussion about life's big questions, and introduced me to great thinkers like Ravi Zacharias, Tim Keller, and Alistair Begg. Most would have given up on me, but like Cheryl, he never did. In most respects—as it is for Cheryl—my tribute to Carl is in the book. Among the lessons of my journey is that an extraordinary life is possible when someone is blessed, as I am, with an extraordinary wife, terrific children, wonderful parents, and at least one friend like Carl.

INTRODUCTION

This story is about a journey—my journey, but perhaps everyone's journey. In many ways, this brief memoir is about my midlife crisis. It is not, though, about purchasing an expensive, foreign sports car or about a dangerous attraction to a woman fifteen years my junior. Rather, it's about the realization that I had to confront certain issues impacting my health. I knew that if I did not do something very soon, I would face a mountain of challenges as I headed into the later years of my life.

I was about to turn fifty and had so much I still wanted to do. With perhaps too much pride, I believed that I had accomplished a lot, but I hoped to do much more, particularly many things time had not yet permitted. I wanted to spend more time with my wife, Cheryl. I wanted to travel. I wondered about a second or encore career. I became increasingly aware, however, that if I continued to ignore my increasingly poor health, I would never get to do many of the things to which I looked forward.

At this same time, maybe in part because of my health and age, my focus turned often to exploring or wondering about some of life's big questions—particularly, those focused on meaning and destiny. Not to be too cliché, but I was asking myself, "What's it all about?" and "What's really important?" Significantly, this meant also considering my religious faith. For someone who never really gave much thought to being fifty years old, the recognition of that milestone appears to have intensified my interest in this next phase of my life. These were not, however, desperate or disturbing thoughts. In fact, I had come to believe earnestly that this next decade might well be the very best years—old enough to have some experience and perspective but still young enough to scale some new heights.

While this time may not have been an urgent crisis, it was a period of intense introspection accompanied by a medical situation that was inconsistent with the hopes and dreams still laid out for me. In short, the time had come to do something. I made an appointment with a doctor. With less surprise than learning that the sun rises in the east, I was told I needed to eat better, to start exercising again, and to lose weight. Running, I thought, would probably be something I could do and enjoy. In fact, a few years earlier (during one of my short-lived recommitments to "get in shape—once and for all"), I had thought that running a marathon the year I turned fifty would be quite an accomplishment.

This book is about embarking on and trying to run a marathon at mid-life, but it is also about life's long run—exploring life's biggest questions, questions that everyone inevitably faces. It is, then, about the race that is set out before each of us.

—Bruce Matson

Every morning in Africa, a gazelle wakes up.

It knows it must outrun the fastest lion or it will be killed.

Every morning in Africa, a lion wakes up.

*It knows that it must run faster than the slowest gazelle,
or it will starve.*

It doesn't matter whether you're a lion or a gazelle

when the sun comes up you'd better be running.

—Author Unknown

CHAPTER I

HITTING THE WALL

The problem with man's unbelief is not the absence of evidence, but the suppression of it.

—Ravi Zacharias

Randy and I began the race together. The morning air was brisk, and the day was highlighted by bright sun and steady ocean breeze—a pretty nice day for a run. At the halfway mark we were still running together, but I recognized the pace was probably too much for me. Randy was the far stronger and better conditioned runner. I told him to go ahead as I backed down my pace for the second 13 miles—hoping that I'd at least be able to finish. Randy finished with a time (in just under three hours) that qualified him to run on Patriots Day in Boston the following year. I ran out of gas and had to walk some in the last five miles. Runners call it "hitting the wall," the point at which physically you feel as though you have nothing left.

Despite hitting the wall, I had met my goals: I had finished, and I wasn't last. In fact, although an entire hour behind Randy, I finished in just under four hours, a respectable time.

That race was the Shamrock Marathon in Virginia Beach, Virginia. The year was 1978, and I was twenty-one years old.

Twenty-eight years later *I hit the wall again*. Physically, my ability to cover twenty-six miles at any pace above a walk was essentially nonexistent. Not only had I not exercised seriously for far too many years, but I was clearly overweight. In fact, during the summer of 2006, my six-foot frame tipped the scales a couple of times at over 260 pounds—not something to be proud of. I needed to do something, but I resisted.

Some friends and colleagues expressed concern indirectly about my health by suggesting I join them for a workout or a run. A couple of my law partners, who routinely ran the Richmond marathon, actually encouraged me to run the next one or maybe the Virginia Beach half-marathon they also ran in each year. In retrospect, these suggestions bordered on the absurd.

I understand why addicts find that meaningful change is impossible until they admit their situation is unmanageable and life threatening. Twelve-step programs call it "hitting bottom." For me it was hitting the wall. Like alcoholics, I had gotten worse—could I get better?

Once in a while I would read an article about Type II diabetes—it sure sounded a lot like me. An assistant in our office published an article in our law firm newsletter about sleep apnea. It sure sounded a lot like me. I put this article in the top drawer of my desk. I could focus on it sometime later, I decided. I suppressed this warning and others by convincing myself that when life and work were a little less hectic or whenever I *really* wanted to, I could just change my eating habits or return to a rigorous exercise regime.

I had a physical a few years earlier and was told I had high cholesterol and high blood pressure. I was supposed to have a follow-up visit, but I cancelled the appointment because I was too busy at work. While that was true, I also I didn't want to face what I sensed was there. I knew my diet and exercise were a problem, but I just wanted to ignore them. I wanted to suppress the evidence right in front of my face. My wife, Cheryl, can confirm that far too often I adopt the "if I ignore it, it will go away" approach to problems.

In truth, my ability to ignore what was right in front of me could only be described as both prodigious and idiotic. A year earlier my brother, two years my senior, died as a result of complications from diabetes. My relationship with my brother had been rocky at best. We had vastly different interests—mine had been baseball, basketball, football, and girls; his had been music, theater, and writing. With little in common, we lived in the same house as kids; we fought at times but generally ignored each another. With age, as we completed college, some level of maturity helped us to be civil and look for some common ground; but with him in New York City and me in Virginia, we had few opportunities and even fewer efforts to spend meaningful time together.

I knew that in many respects I represented much of what created pain for him. He was highly intelligent, creative, and remarkably talented. In society's eyes, however, I had the hallmarks of acceptance and success. I had been captain of the baseball team, while he never seemed to get the part he wanted in the school play. I was married with two beautiful children and a partner in a successful law firm; he lived alone and labored in vain for years, hoping to get one of his musicals produced on Broadway. The depth of my brother's contempt but his desire to connect was brought home when, after his death, my sister found a handwritten letter he had written to me but had never mailed. Every time I reread it, I cry. Here is what he wrote.

Bruce—

  As a brother I have failed you miserably. I gave myself many safe excuses for not being close to you and we have been hiding behind these excuses for too long. I am/was surprised at how much you had grown while I was away. Still I made no attempt to be closer to you. I am jealous of you for many reasons. Your athletic prowess— your popularity—your success. You also anger me—you have no flexibility—you must learn that bending is necessary. You must think, and realize that someone else may have an opinion. I must realize that you have an opinion that is also viable. . . . Perhaps if we could each take one step in the right direction and be friends . . .

Your brother,

Jeff

As we aged, we got along better; but whatever steps we took toward each other were too infrequent and too reserved. Here was a relationship, like my health, that I had ignored far too much. A meaningful relationship with my brother was now impossible. Doing something about my health was not.

Despite Jeff's premature death, I seemed incapable of putting two and two together and understanding that it should have been a wake-up call for me. In a small defense of myself (that's what lawyers do—make up excuses or try to convince people that red is really green), the most intense run of cases in my career coincided with my declining health. I handled three significant Chapter 11 bankruptcy filings. I worked long and hard hours but jumped up in profile, profits, and power. And what more does a lawyer want and need than those three big "Ps." I became one of our firm's biggest producers. I grew a practice from two to twenty attorneys. I served on important management committees at the firm. I was very well compensated. Most would probably say I was successful; many would say I was very successful—at least by some measures.

If this were some simplistic, cliché-ridden tale of being lost and then found, the story would also involve a confession of how I had essentially sold my body and soul to work, money, and recognition. Perhaps it would include how I cheated on my wife, abused alcohol, and how I never thought about a relationship with God.

But that was not my situation. Despite my paper chase, I tried to understand what I thought was most important in life, what gave some meaning to our day-to-day existence, and what I believed about God. I worked hard to be engaged in our daughters' lives. I coached their soccer teams and rarely missed a concert or an athletic contest. In more recent years, I had begun to focus more on what I referred to as the "things that endure" and began to realize more and more that those things that seemed most valuable—what we should spend our time worrying about, *really* worrying about—were marriage, family, and friends. These relationships, not a big home or professional achievement, would endure.

After twenty-plus years of trying to succeed in a law practice and be a good husband and father, while pursuing some hobbies (golf and writing about golf), something inevitably had to give. For me, it was my health. This particularly bothered my ego because in my pre-law life, my identity was mostly as an athlete—a decent high school baseball and soccer player, a vigorous backpacker and canoe guide, and someone who had completed two 26-mile marathons in college.

Hitting the wall and making changes began in, of all places, my bed.

For years I had been notorious for snoring loudly. That typically disturbed others' sleep, not mine. I snored happily away, and they woke up tired. But over time, I began suffering from chronic fatigue. I was having trouble staying awake on the twenty-minute commute from our home to my office. One morning I fell asleep and bumped the car in front of me—thankfully it happened in very slow moving traffic, and no harm was done. Often I found myself nodding off in highway traffic. On road trips to and from Roanoke or Alexandria I struggled to stay awake. While I had snored for many years, my exhaustion became increasingly severe. I was falling asleep in meetings at work, even with colleagues across the desk from me. I found staying awake at a movie, concert, play, or any other evening activity where I had to sit, watch and listen nearly impossible.

I can't say I wasn't warned. Friends who shared a room with me during a guy's golf trip would make comments, but I was in some form of denial. Cheryl was concerned but remarkably patient. She would try to get me to call her on a long drive home so she could talk to me during the trip and try to keep me awake. She did this without any unasked-for advice about what I should or should not be doing—simply out of concern and love.

In the spring of 2006, something finally caused me to say to Cheryl, "I should go have one of those sleep tests." I'm sure she was more than relieved, but she was neither exasperated nor judgmental with me, just supportive, probably hoping, and maybe praying, that I would really go.

Almost six months after this epiphany, after I jumped thorough all the health insurance hoops, I visited a converted one-floor home on the edge of a subdivision to be monitored all night by various machines, electronics, and cameras. Big Brother *was* watching. The sleep technician, who minimized the boredom by telling me about his upbringing in the Philippines and his immigration to the States, took a good hour to hook various parts of my body to all the electronic sensors and then bid me a good night.

The process was painless and seemed to pass quickly. Of course, just like every night, I was exhausted, so falling asleep, even under these circumstances with wires attached, was easy. And while I snored away, the sleep clinic recorded my breathing, heart rate, blood oxygen levels, and other vital signs.

A few weeks later I met with Dr. Rakesh Soud who shared the rather frightening results on just one sheet of paper. I had, he said, "a severe case of sleep apnea." During my night at the clinic, I had stopped breathing an average of thirty to forty times an hour. "Apnea" is a Greek word meaning "without breath," and I was. During one hour I had stopped breathing seventy times. Other than that (in the same sense as, "Other than that, Mrs. Lincoln, how did you enjoy the play?"), I guess it had been a pleasant evening.

Dr. Soud also walked me through sleep "architecture"—what normal, restful sleep should look like and what mine looked like. Let's just say for a serious student of the game of golf, that watching Greg Norman lose a six-stroke lead on Masters' Sunday or Tom Watson's 2009 British Open playoff loss was more encouraging. We should all look away from serious automobile accidents. Yet, I needed to face my train wreck of a lifestyle.

I was not at the diagnosis. I was surprised that my condition was so dangerous and my situation so severe. I was mor[e] anxious as I waited a month till I could get in for another at the clinic. At this pajama party, the lab technician—n from the Philippines—spent the first two or three hour ...he night interrupting my sleep as he tried a variety of nasal and full face masks designed to feed forced air down my windpipe in an effort to keep it open for an entire night. Hopefully, the right equipment would curtail my apnea episodes so I could have uninterrupted sleep.

A few weeks later, Dr. Soud showed me another 8½ by 11 sheet of paper that showed the fits and starts as we tried to find the right mask and mix of pressure and oxygen. Once the combination was right, I could see the dramatic improvement in the quality of my sleep. He really didn't have to show me the results from the second night; as you might say, he had me at "severe."

So off I went to my local home health care supplier for my very own "Continuous Positive Airway Pressure or CPAP machine with matching facemask and supplemental oxygen.

I got my new toys home and set them up preparing to make a change. I figured I didn't really have any choice—remember my situation was "severe," and, by now, the guilt and embarrassment of having abused myself for so long had set in decidedly.

After the first week of figuring out how to arrange my body during sleep so as not to break the mask's seal, I recall saying to Cheryl, "I can't say that it is pleasant, but if it was this tolerable after a week, I think in a few weeks it will be pretty easy."

The impact was almost immediate. I felt rested. Cheryl said I looked much better. People at work noticed and commented. One friend said I had actually looked *gray*, but that better color had now returned. And I was no longer falling asleep in meetings or while driving or at our daughters' piano or violin recitals.

At the same time, whether from guilt, fear, obligation, or something else, I "knew" I had to do something about my diet and exercise or, as my health insurance salesman said, "nutrition" and "physical activity." I committed to getting a doctor, having a complete physical, and facing whatever else I had done to myself.

Jim Mumper was a doctor I knew from our old neighborhood. I thought I'd be comfortable with him, and he agreed to add me as a patient. I had a couple of months before my appointment, and, embarrassed by my weight, I thought I could get going on losing some heft. I started to walk on a treadmill at the YMCA a couple of times a week and eating nothing but fruit and cottage cheese for lunch most days. I lost a few pounds, but my official, fully clothed weight at the weigh-in on January 2 was 258 pounds.

Talk about New Year's resolutions. As Dr. Mumper noted, "You're pretty brave to come in here right after the holidays." Brave was not what I was thinking. I had a four-hour physical, advanced blood work, and, a few days later, a heart scan. A week later, we met to go over the results.

While he never used the word "severe," Dr. Mumper confirmed that I was a walking, Type-II diabetes time bomb—I was overweight (with excess "belly fat"—boy, I hated the sound of that, but it was obviously true) with high blood pressure and high cholesterol.

Sitting there, my mind raced. Rather than go back into denial, I had to face facts. Coincidentally, I was having these discussions with physicians a few months before my fiftieth birthday. We discussed nutrition and physical activity. I bragged about my recent discipline of just eating fruit for lunch. "That's pretty good," he responded, "but fruit has lots of sugar." Feeling a bit frustrated and unenlightened, I asked, "What type of diet, I mean nutrition plan, would you recommend?" He suggested the South Beach Diet.

I figured the South Beach Diet was some fad that went along with Botox treatments, but on the way home I bought the book and read it. A week later I went shopping to start Phase I of the SBD. I learned a lot, followed the diet, and started on an exercise program. Despite hitting the wall physically, I was convinced that my next decade could be the best yet—old enough to have some wisdom but young enough to accomplish much.

I had always found running generally enjoyable, so I decided to try to run as my primary form of exercise. I thought I would work toward running in Richmond's big ten-kilometer race in the spring—the Monument Avenue 10K. I *knew* this resolution would be different—I would keep to this diet and would enjoy developing an exercise routine. But I had said those things before.

A couple of years earlier, I had thought (I had kept this thought to myself) that a great way to celebrate turning fifty would be to complete another marathon—26.2 miles. I had done it before, albeit twenty-eight years earlier, so why not again? Hope does indeed spring eternal.

All thoughts of running a marathon aside, I had a serious and immediate health situation. I had to get going. Winter was upon us, so I went off to the YMCA and climbed back on a treadmill.

HITTING THE WALL II

I'd really rather not talk about it.

—Rosie Ruiz

So, I had sleep apnea. I was overweight. Maybe I wasn't invincible. Maybe our acts or our failures to act have consequences. I could see that simply ignoring this situation would not make it go away. Sleeping like a geriatric patient, breathing with a mask and forced oxygen, certainly humbled me and caused me to do some thinking about where I had been, where I was going, and what was important to me. Questions like these inevitably reach the deepest levels of spirituality, however one defines that. My physical challenges intensified my desire to arrive at some honest conclusions about what was most important in life: What did I value? What did I believe? Why did I believe it? What was I doing to cultivate those "things that endure"?

My parents had raised my older brother, two younger sisters, and me in the Christian tradition. I had been baptized at West Haven Congregational Church. After we moved two years later, we attended North Branford Congregational Church in North Branford, Connecticut. As younger children we recited the Lord's Prayer and occasionally took note of family or friends in need at bedtime. We attended Sunday school and church services regularly.

I remember learning the sixty-six books of the Bible and my third grade Sunday school teacher who captured my imagination with an engaging personality and tales of adventure at high school. His name was Walter Brotherton, and he was the only person who signed my first Bible, the one I received at third grade Sunday school graduation. I still have that Bible with his signature.

We didn't, however, talk much about faith or God at home. Yet family life was very stable and supportive. In fact, my childhood was nearly idyllic. Economically, we were middle class but perhaps trying to take some steps upwards. We took a vacation every summer, had no particular family traumas, and no particular deprivations. At the same time, we did not belong to a country club, had no BMWs for the sixteenth birthday, and enjoyed camping trips in New England instead of European sojourns. Yet, we also seemed to be like everyone else in North Branford, where apparently no one was rich and no one was poor.

The trauma of experimental drug use, racial tensions, anti-war protests, and other issues of the 1960s seemed to pass by our own little Pleasantville of 10,000 people. I don't recall friends' parents getting divorced, older kids getting caught with drugs, or teenage girls getting pregnant. Although our former babysitter crashed his vehicle at high speed under the influence of alcohol in a near fatal accident, I have often told people that my childhood was a like a Coke or Pepsi commercial that features a picnic scene of sack races, egg toss competitions, and the Good Humor man.

Most of the town attended the Roman Catholic church near the junior and senior high schools, the Episcopal church, or, just a quarter-mile down the road from the Episcopalians, our church—North Branford Congregational. By far, the largest contingent went to the Catholic church, but both the Episcopal and Congregational churches had vigorous congregations in the 1960s and 1970s. I still remember at age thirteen responding to a friend's mother when she asked whether our family was Catholic. "We're not even Italian," I said.

Many things in my youth—but far from all—centered on the church. (What I really wanted to do was play shortstop for the New York Yankees, so baseball was clearly my most passionate activity.) We volunteered at church car washes, bake sales, clean-up days, dinners, the big annual auction, and many other activities. My father served on the Church Council and for a year or two was the senior layperson or "president" of the church.

Once when the church needed to raise money for a major capital expense, I learned how much my parents pledged, and it seemed like a lot to me. So I asked my father, a man typically of few words, if we could afford it. He said we had a good year financially and could and should give back more because of it. That made such an impression on me that I've often recalled it when we are deciding on our annual pledge for church.

My brother and I participated regularly in church youth activities. I think at least half the reason I attended was to pursue the girls who also attended. Yet as involved as I was, the group rarely engaged in deep conversations about faith or the big questions of life. Perhaps those happened at the statewide youth gathering or summer Bible camp, activities I missed.

I did, however, attend confirmation class, which after a year led to an examination before the Church Council and finally to confirmation. One of the girls in the class whom I knew well was part of a family that didn't attend our church. She had missed the early years of Sunday school and admitted that she had not read much of the confirmation class materials. So, on the eve of our appearance before the Church Council, she was worried about what they might ask us. I told her that if she read Genesis and one of the gospels, like Matthew, she would know everything she needed. I guess that says more about me than her.

When I arrived at the College of William & Mary in Williamsburg, Virginia for my first year of college, church was not high on my list of priorities. Besides, Williamsburg had no Congregational Churches. Those churches, descended from the original Puritan church established in Boston in 1630, are primarily in New England. I was more concerned about making friends to escape the loneliness of not knowing a single person south of Baltimore. Within a few days of orientation I had become friends with Chip, who would become one of my closest friends and have a profound impact on my exploration of faith.

Chip, who had been raised in the Lutheran Church, and I found ourselves at St. Stephens Lutheran Church on many, if not most Sunday mornings. Perhaps the greatest attraction was St. Stephens' "college room," a very large, carpeted room with a kitchen, fireplace, sofa and easy chairs, and large tables. We were told that the room had been constructed expressly to serve the student population at William & Mary and that we had free access to the room and controlled its use. It quickly became my regular spot for studying.

It may sound as though I was swinging toward religion, but the situation was more complicated. First semester freshman year, I took Philosophy 101, and among the questions we addressed was the existence of God. Chip and I, along with other friends, often would stay up late talking about presidential politics, relationships with girls, and many of life's big questions. Philosophy class gave me plenty of fodder to play devil's advocate for atheism; yet I also had sincere questions about God and faith. Thus, I had both opportunity and motive, as well as the material, to engage friends in questions about God.

Looking back on those college years, I realize that while I had a great time of debate and exploration and attended St. Stephens regularly, I did not really make spiritual progress. I met Cheryl during our last semester at William & Mary. Since we hadn't met before, our friends and college experiences were almost completely different. But we began to date and even went to church together a few times before graduation. I am still haunted by the memory of a drive we took on the Blue Ridge Parkway where something about the Bible came up, and I mocked what I considered her hopelessly naïve belief in the literal nature and accuracy of some of the stories recorded in Genesis.

On the other hand, my advisor had recently converted to Catholicism, which caused me to wonder about my own faith commitments. In a survey of "American Intellectual History," he had us read Thomas Merton's *Seven Story Mountain,* and he gave me a copy of Sheldon Vanauken's *A Severe Mercy* as a graduation present. Faith was definitely on his mind, and, from time to time, it was on my mind as well.

After graduation, Chip and I, along with a third friend, took the classic backpack tour of Western Europe. The trip was amazing for many reasons with plenty of material for a separate book. But as to my faith, although we visited many churches and cathedrals including Saint Chappelle, Cologne, St. Peter's, and the Vatican Museums and even attended a Wednesday service led by Pope Paul II, I do not recall my thoughts or my conversations centering on questions of faith despite the omnipresence of Christian symbols all around us. I did miss Cheryl terribly, and when I returned to the States in August, I moved to Williamsburg to be near her and to figure out what we were going to do and what I was going to do with myself and my college degree.

Cheryl worked nearby in Newport News. We visited as often as we could, but mostly on the weekends. Eating dinner in my efficiency while trying to figure out "Who shot J.R.?" became our regular activity. After waiting tables and then, after being unemployed, I needed to focus on a real future, so I took the LSAT, hoping to head to law school. My friend Carl was still at William & Mary at this time. We spent many evenings discussing our futures, our girlfriends, and our faith, Carl patiently listening to my questions and doubt.

Many things changed that summer. Chip, who also continued to listen to my inquiries about God, was preparing to enter seminary. I worked on a peanut farm in Southside Virginia. I struggled with issues of belief, but ultimately silenced the voices of doubt during the summer of 1980, shortly before starting law school. I also asked Cheryl to marry me.

An old saying is that in law school they scare you to death in the first year, work you to death in the second year, and bore you to death in the third year. As a former pledge student of that fraternity, I can say that simple formula contains much truth. Unsure how well I would compete, my first year is a bit of a blur. Cheryl and I decided to get married after that first year. So in May 1981, we were married by a Catholic priest in the Wren Chapel on the William & Mary campus (when the Bruton Parish cross was still on the altar).

For the rest of law school and the first few years of married life, Cheryl and I attended Catholic services in Williamsburg and then in Richmond where I had a judicial clerkship, though I never became a Catholic. After that one-year job, I took a position with a law firm in Norfolk, and we moved to Newport News. Coincidentally (or was it providentially?), Chip also moved to begin his career as an associate pastor at Trinity Lutheran Church, which became our church until we moved back to Richmond two years later.

In Richmond we attended Christ Lutheran on the North Side of the city where Chip's friend, Jim Mauney, was the young, dynamic pastor. He was so effective, in fact, that shortly after we joined, he was called to be an assistant to the bishop of the Virginia Synod of the Lutheran Church in America. Nonetheless, we stayed and have been members at Christ Lutheran ever since. And Pastor Mauney has since become the bishop of the Virginia Synod.

Christ Lutheran is a modest, middle-class congregation. Richmond's growth has been to the west and south of the city, which leaves the "North Side" as more of a transitional area. At least three other Lutheran Churches are closer than our twenty-five-minute drive to Woodman Road, but Christ has become our church home, a wonderful group of people and families. Many pitch in to teach Sunday school, play hand bells, serve on Church Council, work on repairs, participate in fundraisers, serve as ushers, volunteer in the choir, and count the offering. We never really know where every dollar is going to come from, but each year, somehow, we seem able to meet our expenses.

Not that everything is perfect with Christ Lutheran, though. In retrospect, Cheryl and I have wondered if we let our children down because of the poor attention paid to youth programs. Like many small churches, a minority does most of the heavy lifting. Cheryl, for instance, has taught Sunday school for the younger children and coordinated the volunteer schedule for "junior church" for fifteen years. That includes covering for any volunteer who did not show up, something that happened so often that for many years Cheryl rarely remained in church for the sermon. I recall Pastor Mauney cautioning me not to get burned out too soon when a few members of the congregation approached me about serving on the Church Council.

Yet Cheryl, our two girls, and I went to church religiously— meaning almost every Sunday. I served as a lector, an usher, a trustee, and a member of the Church Council; and I helped in various capital campaigns and other church projects.

Despite my church involvement, I still struggled with a number of questions about faith. I had practical questions, such as what is the proper level of giving and should we be tithing. I was blessed with significant income and wanted, as my father had said, to give back in some way for what I had been so fortunate to receive (or is it "earn"?). But I also had tougher, ultimate questions. I recited either the Apostles' Creed or the Nicene Creed each Sunday, but did I really believe what I said I believed? And if I believed, why did I believe?

In trying to wrap myself around these questions, I had a few spiritual guides including Cheryl, who has been a remarkable example of faithfulness and living a committed, selfless life. I know no one who better lives out the Christian values of humility, service, patience, kindness, and integrity. She has always quietly encouraged me in faith.

Carl has been with me since college and the beginnings of my struggles to talk through many of these perplexing questions. Over the years he has introduced me to great writers and thinkers, and shared books and tapes on most of the questions with which

I have struggled. He first introduced me to Ravi Zacharias's book *Can Man Live Without God?*—a book I have consulted often when trying to gain some understanding of life's ultimate question.

At the same time, I considered myself a rational, self-reliant man. I readily adopted the Protestant work ethic and the belief that you could pull yourself up by your own bootstraps. I found these Yankee values from my upbringing to be admirable. I picked fruit, delivered newspapers, bused tables, and worked construction all before college—anything to earn some money, even though I seemed incapable of parting with any of it.

Our family has had some good laughs about this "Scottish" tendency, particularly in my youth when I recounted a story about my stinginess. When I was in fifth grade, my family took a trip to Florida. I brought along a five-dollar bill for my personal spending money. I loved to eat coconut and thought I might like to buy a "real" one while in the Sunshine State. We made some stops at places for souvenirs where I could have purchased a coconut (which cost 25 cents). I put off the decision each time, however, and held onto my money. In fact, I so thoroughly deferred the purchase that I returned to Connecticut with my $5.00 bill intact. More recently, when our daughter Brooke seemed to exhibit a hint of having inherited that same gene while considering some modest purchase, Cheryl told her, "Just buy the coconut". The expression is now part of our family lexicon, like most lines from the remake of "The Parent Trap" ("Don't tell me you're going to end your rotten streak and suddenly be nice to me" and "You're going to *adopt* Meredith").

I have almost always believed that, if given a chance and enough time, I could figure out or accomplish just about anything if I set my mind (and, if necessary, my back) to it. For me this fierce strain of independence and self-reliance was the key to any success I had achieved. Thus, when considering questions or doubt about God, I thought I could figure it all out if I just applied myself, if I could gather all the facts and evidence and consider all the arguments. Yet, as I was beginning to think more deeply about belief and faith, such rigorous self-reliance didn't seem to be the best recipe for developing a deep, Christian conviction. Didn't "faith" suggest belief in something despite a lack of solid evidence? Isn't that what we mean by a "leap of faith"? As I pondered these questions, my emphasis on, if not devotion to, self-reliance appeared to be antithetical to honest belief—acceptance of God seemed to be an acknowledgement of my need for something other than myself. And I have always been pretty confident "I could handle it" myself—regardless of what "it" was. Thus, I figured that, at best, I was a curious, but reluctant Christian.

As I approached my fiftieth birthday, Christ Lutheran was looking for ways to focus on an enhanced ministry for children and youth to attract, hopefully, new families to the congregation. Cheryl served on a search committee to locate a junior or youth pastor. I wondered if that was still the best church for the family and me. I also seemed to be questioning what I really believed. Was my uneasiness merely dissatisfaction with our church or something more fundamental? As I recited one of the creeds each Sunday, I started to wonder if I really believed what I was saying.

Except for the long-term relationships and our twenty years as members, I almost certainly would have urged Cheryl to consider making a move. Encouraged and led by my college friend, Carl, I began to listen more regularly to sermons and to read some materials that happened to be by Presbyterian ministers. Their words captured my attention and I found myself wondering if the Presbyterian Church might be a better place for us, particularly as I recognized just how many of our local friends and acquaintances went to one of its local churches.

At about this time, with a variety of these thoughts and questions running around in my mind, I visited my parents in Florida to play in my father's member-guest golf tournament, which I had done for a number of years. During that visit, my mother recounted their recent activities with their friends—bowling, bridge, golf, shared meals, dinners out, etc. In particular, she recalled a recent visit with another couple during which these friends indicated that they were atheists. In the telling of the story itself and her reaction to what she learned, my mother appeared surprised and disappointed to learn this. For me, the obvious implication was that she (and my father) believed in God, which itself took me a little by surprise (mostly because the issue had never come up among us, and they had attended church little after their children left home). Unfortunately, I let this opening pass without engaging them in a discussion of the questions I had, but it did cause me to note the coincidence that this revelation would arise at this time, as I was seriously concerned about what it was that I believed.

Chapter 3

Beginning to Run

Many shall run to and fro, and knowledge shall increase.

—Daniel 12:4 (ESV)

In high school I was a fair athlete; in fact, sports were essentially my identity. I played soccer, baseball, and one season of basketball (and then took up skiing). As for running, I ran only to train and to practice for those sports—and for two months senior year when I joined a particular girl for laps around the track during our free period out of motives that had nothing to do with fitness. Running distances just seemed too hard. I was amazed when a childhood friend who wasn't very good at team or ball sports (and whose father regularly reminded him about those deficiencies) began running. Sometimes he ran between his home and school. I couldn't believe he was running four or five miles at a time. His efforts paid off, though, and he became one of the best cross-country runners in the state.

In college I played club soccer and various intramural sports. I also did a lot of backpacking and canoeing, including competitive, intercollegiate canoe racing (I know, you learn something new every day), but again, no running. That is, not until my junior year.

In the fall of 1977, Randy, my good friend, fraternity brother, and roommate at William & Mary, began running and was going for four- and five-mile runs after classes. That seemed like very long distances to me. When I asked why he was running so much, he replied, "I'm training to run a marathon."

"Wow!" I said. "What a great thing to accomplish." I was completely sincere. I considered running a marathon to be an extraordinary accomplishment.

I continued to laud his efforts regularly until he finally interrupted me, "There's no reason you can't do it too." I scoffed at the idea, but quickly realized he was serious. I gave the notion some thought.

I liked challenges, taking pride in things like having climbed most of the highest peaks in the Eastern United States I don't recall how long I thought about the possibility, but I do recall thinking that running a marathon would be an amazing accomplishment. So, sometime in late 1977, I started running, and I told Randy I would run the Shamrock Marathon with him in March.

On a crisp, cool and somewhat windy Saturday, Randy and I drove the hour to Virginia Beach and completed the Shamrock's 26.2 miles. That fall we ran a second race, the Marine Corps Marathon in Washington, D.C., which boasted a field of more than 3,000 runners as the country enjoyed its first running boom.

After college graduation, I didn't run until law school, where I would run two or three miles just to get away from the library. I ran a 5K "ambulance chase," a fundraiser I think. I sprinted the last quarter mile of the race to finish just ahead of a good friend with whom I would compete in any pickup sport we could find time to enjoy. And, while preparing for the bar exam, I routinely would run around Lake Matoaka at William & Mary—a mental release of about two miles.

After Cheryl and I were married and I was doing my post-graduation law clerkship, I would run a couple of miles many evenings while Cheryl would go to aerobics class. Always interested in challenges, I even ran home from work a few times—a nine-mile trek. But once I got a real job with a law firm, I don't recall ever going for a run again, although I played squash often, exercised regularly, and was in fair shape. Five years

later, the birth of our first daughter put the nail in the exercise
and running coffin. By the end of 2006 when I resolved to do
something about my health, eighteen years had passed since I
had done any significant or regular running.

Part of my "New Year's Resolution" in 2007 was to try to run in
Richmond's Monument Avenue 10K race, typically held the last
Saturday of March or the first Saturday in April. That gave me
about three months to try to get ready to complete (that's *complete*,
not compete in) the 6.2 mile race. I signed up for the local YMCA
10K Training Team, which was scheduled to begin in the middle
of January. This was a ten-week training program to help runners,
especially novices like me, get ready for the Monument Avenue
race.

My fitness was so pathetic; I thought I'd better get started
before the formal program began. I wasn't sure how far I could
run, but I knew it wasn't 6.2 miles or even 3.1 miles for that matter.
The winter weather made running outside difficult, so I started
by going to the nearby YMCA to walk on a treadmill. I would
try to walk thirty to forty-five minutes changing the speed and
the incline to get a good workout and to break up the monotony
of just walking at one speed for a long time. After a few weeks I
started adding a few minutes of running into the routine. I got
home from the Y one of those first few weeks and proudly told
Cheryl that I had run five straight minutes! It sounds pathetic
now, but I had to start somewhere.

I continued walking and running two to four times a week into
January. I even worked my treadmill routine into out-of-town
business trips. Before long, the day came for the first 10K Training
Team meeting, around the corner from our house at Collegiate
School. I was intimidated to show up, not certain that I could
really do this. Thankfully, the number of participants was large,
and I could gain some anonymity by getting lost in the crowd even
if a few friends were there, too. After some introductory remarks,
our training team coaches led us in some warm-up exercises and
off we went for a one-mile run.

For whatever reason, I *knew* I could run one mile, and I did—not terribly fast, but without walking and without finishing last. While I knew I could run one mile, I had no idea if I could do two, which was on the training schedule for the next Saturday. After that we would be up to three miles in what seemed to be no time.

That first two-mile run proved to be difficult. I handled the first half fine but felt my strength fading shortly thereafter. I slowed a little but didn't stop to rest or walk—my ego led me to think that such behavior was simply unacceptable. With one of the coaches yelling encouragement at the last turn, I picked up my pace and finished with a quicker step. We would run two miles again the next week, and then we'd add another mile to that. Two miles had been pretty hard, so how would I be able to run three?

When that Saturday in February rolled around, the task was relatively straight forward, if not simple: complete three miles with the novice running group at whatever pace would get the job done. I was both anxious and eager to get going. (For many, the words are synonymous. Not for my family! And, apparently, not according to *Webster's*. I'm not sure anyone in our immediate family will forget the distinction; the two words—"anxious" and "eager"—having been the subject of a particularly memorable pre-test tutoring session by Cheryl for one of our girls.) Years had passed since I had been able to run that far, but I did. It was a milestone, an accomplishment, a feeling I would repeat as I tried to run four and five miles and later as I tried to go even farther. Here is how I recorded my thoughts about that morning:

> *A very cold morning. I stretched with the group, but was eager to get going. Finally, we were off. My law partner and his friend were a hundred yards ahead. I decided on a comfortable, easy pace. I focused on the potential accomplishment. Like the tortoise and the hare, my steady pace led me to pass my friends and most others. With about a mile to go we ran up a gentle rise. I could begin to feel fatigue, but thought I could finish and I did.*

The following Saturday we were to run the same distance.

My "anxiety" about being able to finish had diminished. I did my miles very early and without the team so I could make it to a Church Council meeting. My brief record of that run states: "Started slow and easy. Quickly got comfortable and relaxed. Not too hard—actually enjoyed the run and recalled the meditative aspect of a good run." It seemed as though I was—pardon the pun—off and running. I was making some progress. With some confidence came greater eagerness. Maybe I could follow this program.

The training team provided a schedule of runs to do during the week between Saturdays. Following it is nearly a sure-fire way to be ready to run the 10K when race day comes. The plan called for running two or three times a week for a distance that was a little less than the mileage for the Saturday group run. In week six, for example, the training schedule had us run 2.5 miles on Monday and 4.5 miles on Wednesday in preparation for the group run of five miles that Saturday.

I didn't make every run every week, but I did most of them—maybe seventy or eighty percent compliance. I ran some on treadmills and some on neighborhood streets. The reason may have been confidence, improving fitness, or just because the weather was improving, but I soon ran much less on treadmills and more outdoors.

Not every Saturday run was the same; some were more difficult than others. One week early in the program, I got halfway through the day's run and just wanted to quit. Then I focused on a woman just ahead of me; she who had been just ahead of me for most of the run. I settled in behind her at an easy pace and thought if I could only stay with her, I could finish. I really wanted to stop, but I kept right with her, so much so that with a half a mile to go, I assured her that I was not a stalker. She acknowledged her doubts, laughed, and a few minutes later we congratulated each other when we arrived back at the school together.

On the Saturdays that I couldn't make the training team workouts, I tried to get out anyway. When our family visited New

York City for Spring Break in March just a few weeks before the 10K event, Brooke joined me for a five-mile run in Central Park. Five miles was pretty far (and I didn't want my far-better-fit daughter see me struggle); but the temperature was good, and when I realized I'd be able to finish, I was thankful I could enjoy that time together. It was one of those "things that endure."

The breakthrough moment was learning to run at a pace that kept me working but not winded. To do that, I concentrated on my legs and would ask myself, "Are my legs tired? Am I just running too fast for my ability and getting winded?" When I concentrated on my legs and realized they were not unduly fatigued, I found that I could keep going if my pace was reasonable for my wind capacity. That's how I began to find my pace. And I seemed to be able to keep that pace fairly constant. In fact, after one run in the middle of the program, a fellow runner came over to me and said, "I hope you don't mind, but I always follow you on these runs because you keep such a steady pace." Most Saturdays I would head out in the middle of the pack, not trying to go out too fast, but staying at my pace. By the end of the run, I would finish toward the front, my tortoise pace ultimately overcoming some of the novice hares.

A new runner, like a new parent, gets a lot of unsolicited advice. I heard much about the benefits and horrors of running on a treadmill. Some swear by the convenience. One of my law partners has trained for three or four marathons primarily on his treadmill. When the time comes for long runs training for a marathon, he watches two full-length movies while running. Others find treadmills just too boring and monotonous. With the growth of running, manufacturers put in the requisite research; so many treadmills are designed for less severe impact and presumably fewer injuries than running on sidewalks or pavement.

Although I prefer running outdoors, the treadmill is a great tool to supplement training. At times running outside just isn't possible or wise. Bitter cold is bad, and sweltering heat is an even more formidable enemy. At a conference in Scottsdale, Arizona I hoped to get in my training runs between sessions. But the temperature was around 100 degrees, so I ran in an air-conditioned fitness room looking out over the pool and the desert. Sometimes it's not easy or convenient to find a good, local running route when traveling. Jumping on a treadmill, even if in some small, interior fitness room helped to keep me honest with my training schedules.

A couple of years after I started training for my first 10K race, I was still running. Many times friends or colleagues would comment, "I don't know how you find the time. I'm just too busy to fit running into my week." Although often tempted to suggest that my schedule of work and other commitments are more intense and inflexible than theirs, I would say simply, "It's hard, but you just have to find what works for you." After fifty years, I've learned with relative certainty that most of us do what we want to do. We do those things that are high on our list of priorities.

Initially, running was something I did when I found a window of time—sometimes in the morning, sometimes on a Saturday afternoon. When I committed to the 10K training team, I had to get two or three runs in a week before the long Saturday run. I decided to run first thing in the morning, which I usually did. When I was tired, I'd stay in bed and say to myself, "I'll get out at lunch." That approach just didn't work. Rarely did I run during lunch, in the afternoon, or in the evening when I refused to pull myself out of bed in the morning. I soon realized that I had to schedule time to run, and I had to make it a priority very early in the morning. My health depended on it.

Even after my commitment to get up early and run became a routine, getting from the bed to the street was still a challenge. What helped was getting up even earlier, something I continue to this day. My time window was such that I needed to be back by 7 a.m. to make sure our teenage daughter was up for school and to prepare her breakfast. So I have a cup of coffee at 5 a.m., enjoy thirty minutes or so of personal or quiet time, and then

I head out. This works very well for me. Individuals just have to be honest with themselves and design an approach that allows them to predictably and consistently make time to run. More than anything, it has to become a priority. If your run is the first thing you give up when schedule problems arise or if your excuses to skip are questionable, you may never make it.

As I continued with my training program and the Saturday morning runs, I started to show better discipline. I was making running a priority, even taking running clothes and usually getting my run in when traveling on business. When I visited my parents to play in my father's member-guest golf tournament in Florida and had to miss a group run, I had my father map out a local three- or four-mile route for me.

All of which is to say, that while I still had weight to lose and a few health issues to monitor, I had made real progress. I had begun to take steps toward permanent changes in my life. I had not run very far, not even the 10K yet. But I had reason to think that I might actually get there.

CHAPTER 4

BEGINNING THE RACE
(PHILOSOPHY 101)

When I got to the starting line, I didn't even know where to stand.

—Grete Waitz

Regardless of the mileage, running alone provides a wonderful time to think and reflect. Some people work out family problems or stresses at work; others try to solve the world's great dilemmas. I found that training runs, particularly when I was alone during the week between Saturdays, were a great time to clear my mind or work things out. Like many people, it is rare with my schedule that I have any significant time to just think.

I continued to be preoccupied by questions about what was most important in life. As the old saying goes, "No one on his deathbed wishes he had spent more time in the office." Even wrapped up with seeking professional success, I could clearly see that relationships with family and friends were far more meaningful and valuable than a hefty investment account or a river house. I had to agree with George Strait as he sings, "Life is not the breath you take, but the moments that take your breath away."

For a few years I took each of our daughters on their own father-daughter weekend. One of the very first of these trips was a weekend with our younger daughter Amy in Williamsburg, including a day at Water Country USA. Even though lightning was threatening, we decided to head to the water park. The questionable weather kept the crowds away, and something kept the lightning away. With no lines to fight, Amy and I exhausted ourselves running from water ride to water ride and from water slide to water slide. After a couple of hours, as we climbed another set of steep steps to get us to the top of the twisting sliding tubes, Amy turned to me and said, "Dad, I didn't know you could have this much fun." Remembering that brings tears to my eyes and, even now, takes my breath away.

So, when I thought more and more about what was *really* important—what really endured, I realized that family, friends, and those relationships are definitely the most precious things in life.

As I trained for the Monument Avenue 10K, many of my early morning runs featured a mental debate about material success and charitable responsibilities. I was troubled by what I began to call the problem of wealth and faith. I earned more money from my law practice at LeClairRyan than I dreamed possible, and I increasingly struggled with the affluence I enjoyed and my impression of what Scripture required. Many passages in the Bible seemed to enjoin Christians to eschew wealth and worldly goods. In particular, I wondered about the meaning of Matthew 19:24: "Again I tell you, it is easier for a rich man to pass through the eye of a needle than to inherit the kingdom of God." Is being a Christian and living the affluent life I was enjoying inconsistent? Didn't Christ tell his disciples to give away all of their worldly possessions?

I wondered whether God might ask me at judgment day why I spent so much of my wealth on myself? While I wasn't contemplating a radical step, I did ask quite seriously—particularly each "pledging season" at our church—just how much we should give to the church and to other causes and how much we should keep. I even started collecting thoughts and materials for a book I considered writing—comparing, contrasting, and trying to extract meaning from the seemingly contradictory biblical treatment of wealth, possessions, and charity.

As I settled into a regular running routine, my focus on wealth and faith became a catalyst for more fundamental questions. As much as I wanted to explore how a wealthy person—perhaps someone like me—could make it through the eye of a needle, I was drawn to even more basic questions, the *most* basic questions. I began to wonder again what I really believed.

Every Sunday the congregation recited either the Apostles' Creed or the Nicene Creed. One morning in the middle of that weekly recital, I asked myself if I really believed what I was saying. Did I really accept as true each of the tenants of the creeds?

APOSTLES' CREED

I believe in God, the Father Almighty,
the Creator of heaven and earth,
and in Jesus Christ, His only Son, our Lord:
Who was conceived by the Holy Ghost,
born of the virgin Mary,
suffered under Pontius Pilate,
was crucified, dead, and buried;
He descended into hell.
The third day He arose again from the dead;
He ascended into heaven,
and sits on the right hand of the Father;
and he shall come to judge the living and the dead.
I believe in the Holy Ghost;
the holy catholic Church;
the communion of saints;
the forgiveness of sins;
the resurrection of the body;
and the life everlasting.
Amen.[1]

I knew almost immediately that I had to answer that question. And if I did not believe those things, how could I attend each week and say that I did? I needed to preserve some fundamental integrity—if not hypocritical, it would just be downright dishonest. I can certainly recall my distaste, if not contempt, for those who said one thing and did another. An old test of integrity or character puts the question this way: What do we do or how do we act when no one is looking?

With these thoughts in mind, I recalled a story I repeated often to friends and others about "my day with the king"—a story about a day I spent with golf legend, Arnold Palmer. (Just as Bruce Springsteen is "The Boss" in the music business, in the golf world, Mr. Palmer is referred to affectionately as "The King.")

A few years before I hit the wall, I was given the opportunity to write the history of the Bay Hill Club in Orlando, Florida, which is owned by Palmer and serves as his winter home. I received a modest writer's fee, but for the opportunity to meet my golf hero, I would have taken the assignment for no compensation. In addition to interviewing Palmer a number of times for the book, I had the opportunity to play golf with him three times. What most of those who asked wanted to know was whether he really was the way he appeared. Essentially, they were asking what Palmer is like when the cameras are off. How does he act when no one is looking?

Although often presumed, rarely does one articulate why he or she is interested in the answers to questions like those. At the core, people want to know if their admiration for people like Warren Buffet or Arnold Palmer is justified. Or might such famous individuals be just as (or more) unbearable and two-faced as many we encounter in life. At the core, we appear to admire integrity, and that is one way to see if our heroes pass the test.

In response to these questions, I usually tell this story (abbreviated here) about "my day with the king." After interviewing Mr. Palmer for a couple of hours in his workshop at Bay Hill, we jumped in his golf cart to drive the four hundred yards to the first tee. We were scheduled to play with his grandson and one of his closest friends. Almost as soon as we left his condo, we drove by an individual carrying a book or a print in a bag. Palmer waved "good morning" to him as he walked in the opposite direction but then asked if I would mind if he stopped for a second. He thought this man might want him to autograph something. So, Palmer excused himself, went back, and confirmed with the individual that he'd catch up with him later. Off we went for a round of golf—me with the king (it still seems surreal).

As we drove through the parking lot that connected the condominiums to the golf course, another person jumped in front of the cart unexpectedly, requiring Mr. Palmer to stop abruptly. The man exclaimed that he was visiting from Kentucky, that his son played high school golf there, and that it would be an enormous honor if his son could meet Mr. Palmer. Without showing an ounce of anger or distraction, Palmer simply responded by saying, "I'm getting ready to play golf here with Mr. Matson, but I'd love to meet your son. You can meet me down at the first tee in a few minutes." As we drove away, I expected Palmer to say something like—"That idiot!" or "Can you believe some people?!" but it was nothing like that. Rather, he apologized to me for the interference.

We drove the final 100 yards to the first tee. Mr. Palmer and I each ordered a hot dog and an "Arnold Palmer" (a drink consisting of half iced tea and half lemonade). We sat together at a picnic table near the first tee with our quick lunch. Within a few moments the dad and son from Kentucky arrived. Mr. Palmer again apologized and excused himself. He shook hands, signed autographs, and posed for photographs. He returned to our table a few minutes later and again apologized. Once more, I saw a perfect opportunity—when the cameras were off and no one was looking—for Palmer to express his exasperation, but he never even suggested it by nuance or body language. So, I do tell my friends who ask that Palmer is just who he appears to be.

Drawn, therefore, to explore my faith, I asked, what did I

really believe? I decided I needed to have the type of integrity between my beliefs and my actions that I witnessed in Arnold Palmer's public and more private moments. I began to listen to some religion courses from The Teaching Company. At the same time, Carl, my college friend, suggested a couple of writers and speakers he thought I might find interesting and useful. Carl would send me CDs and books on topics that he knew would interest me. I began to download podcasts of various messages and sermons on these issues by Christian speakers such as Ravi Zacharias, Alistair Begg, and Tim Keller. Before long, listening to them became routine. During my early morning runs, I would typically listen to one of them as they presented Bible devotionals, commentary on culture from a Christian perspective, philosophy, or apologetics.

When work brought Carl and me to New York City at the same time, Carl took me along to some Bible studies he attended there regularly. Not only did these efforts help to focus my thoughts, but they sparked a preoccupation with these questions. Instead of reading books by David McCullough or Ken Follett, I started to read books on religion, faith and apologetics, the latter of which is a branch of Christian theology focused on the reasons that support a belief in God.

The time on my feet created by my new running discipline provided predictable blocks of time to contemplate and engage in the questions running through my mind. In no particular order, I switched off most mornings among downloads from Zacharias, Keller, and Begg, who challenged and helped organize my thoughts. From their sermons and talks, I gained greater exposure to traditional insight into the Bible as well as into Christian apologetics.

Pastor Alistair Begg, who leads Parkside Church in Cleveland, Ohio, is great at explaining Scripture and the foundational Christian beliefs. Born and raised in Scotland, I had to like him. Not only did I enjoy his modest accent, but having grown up at the same time, his references to music and popular culture are sufficiently out of date to make a direct hit with a fellow Baby Boomer.

Ravi Zacharias is a Christian apologist. Most of his talks addressed a defense of the Christian faith or critiqued modern cultural issues in light of the Christian message. I also learned that an *apologist* is not someone who makes excuses for or is sorry about Christianity but is someone who advocates the reasons why belief in God is the most rational choice given all the evidence. Apologists often quote 1 Peter 3:15, where Peter writes that all followers of Christ should be prepared at all times "to make a defense for the hope that is in us."

Tim Keller, pastor of Manhattan's Redeemer Presbyterian Church, covered insight to Scripture and the Christian faith as well as arguments in defense of a belief in God. As much as I found his content compelling, I was particularly drawn to his presentation style, which I found very orderly and accessible. Probably the lawyer in me liked the structure of his sermons. After an introductory Scripture reading, he begins most talks with something like, "We going to see three things in this story; first...." When I finished listening to a sermon, I'd recognize that he told me what he was going to tell me, then he told me, and then he brought it all together in a cogent summary. Keller's approach was great for "unpacking" (one of his favorite words) difficult issues and confusing Scripture.

One solitary Saturday morning run I decided to go from my home to the James River and back, a 7.1 mile round trip. The run was memorable because if you are inclined to believe in God, it featured one of those moments, one of those "coincidences" that seemed to carry some deeper meaning. Was it a coincidence or God reaching out for me?

I started this run as usual by selecting a podcast on my iPod. After listening to most of his sermon, Alistair Begg recounted that Jesus asked his disciples "Who Do You Say I Am?" (Mark 8:29). I rounded the final curve on the boat access road and came into a clearing. The James River revealed itself on a magnificent morning with the early sunlight accentuating steam rising from the surface of the river. As I spilled onto this exceptionally beautiful sight, I heard Begg asking, "Who do *you* say I am"? Although distracted by the beauty around me, I knew I needed a clear and confident answer to his question. Remaining casual about the issue didn't seem to be an option. It wasn't like someone asking me if I liked chocolate ice cream (about which I am fairly ambivalent). For thousands of years humans have struggled with the question posed by Jesus (and Begg). The answer, at least for most, was life changing. It did not haunt me, but an echo of the question seemed to come back to me often—"Who do you say I am?"

I ran across something British author and scholar C.S. Lewis said that captured the dilemma I faced. Lewis wrote:

> *Christianity, if false, is of no importance and, if true, is of infinite importance. The only thing it cannot be is of moderate importance.*[2]

I had not thought of the issue or articulated it in that way before and it sounded not only correct, but profound.

For almost anyone, the surest way to know that God exists would seem to have a direct, religious experience or revelation. That would settle the question, would it not? Moses had his "burning bush" and Paul his Damascus Road. The Apostles witnessed Christ resurrected after his death on the Cross. Wouldn't that be sufficient, convincing direct evidence? If I could have something like that wouldn't this inquiry be much easier? Sometimes I figured the obstinacy in me would make me much more like (Doubting) Thomas: "Unless I see the nail marks in his hands," he said, "I will not believe it" (John 20:25).

While I didn't seriously expect a grand personal encounter, as a part of the analytical process, I had to acknowledge both the simplicity and logic of such proof. Believing in God would have been easier if I had the same direct evidence or dramatic revelation, but I had no such experience. Yet, I recognized that millions of people reached belief in God without a direct revelation.

I realized that belief in the twenty-first century might be a more difficult than it was for eyewitnesses or others closer to the historical events. Analyzing the question like a lawyer suggested that the current age appeared to provide little or no direct evidence to support a belief in God. Thus, any such belief might take an even greater leap of faith than for required of first century Christians.

On the other hand, Tim Keller said belief in God is rational. That interested me. I had assumed that belief required a "leap of faith," which I understood to mean that ultimate belief in God required the abandonment of reason and logic. After all, didn't belief require acceptance of certain things that could not be verified, things I'd have to take "on faith"? Keller seemed to be suggesting maybe not.

Without really planning it, and before I knew it, I had begun a more intense and systematic exploration. I was on some kind of journey. This was not haphazard wandering. I had a focus and a direction. Without writing an outline or plan, I nonetheless seemed to know where I wanted to start and where, at least initially, I wanted to go.

One of the first sources I consulted was a 24-lecture CD series called an "Introduction to the Philosophy of Religion," which addressed point and counterpoint most of the classical arguments concerning the existence of God. During morning runs, I was trying to analyze the questions and arguments. I found myself back at college in Williamsburg reliving Philosophy 101. The CD series featured professor James Hall, who, coincidentally, is on the faculty at the University of Richmond, just minutes from my home and where I teach a class at the law school. Initially, Hall explained that some have postulated an *a priori* argument to establish the existence of God. *A priori* is Latin for "prior to" and refers to an argument or knowledge that exists prior to and independent of experience. *A priori* arguments don't rely on evidence or experience, but focus on abstract reasoning.

As it applies to God, the argument says that, as a matter of logic, if God's existence is possible, then God must exist. As the eleventh century theologian Anselm of Canterbury argued:

> *God is the greatest idea that can ever be conceived.*
>
> *As a result, God certainly exists in the mind.*
>
> *An idea that exists in reality is greater than an idea that exists only in the mind.*
>
> *If God does not exist in reality, then a greater idea than God exists.*
>
> *Since there exists no idea greater than God, it necessarily follows that God exists.*

This argument is known as the ontological argument. And while it may be intriguing intellectually, it didn't capture my imagination or establish a convincing proof for me. I'm not even sure I really understand it. So I moved on, remembering other arguments from Philosophy 101.

One of the oldest classical arguments, as well as perhaps the most popular and often repeated arguments for the existence of God, is an argument based on the existence of the universe. This is generally referred to as the "cosmological" or "first cause" argument. Simply stated, nothing just happens; everything has a cause. While I doubt she was focused on taking a cosmological stand, Julie Andrews reminded us in *The Sound of Music,* "Nothing comes from nothing; nothing ever could."

The night sky or staring at the "cosmos" has always fascinated me. My family will attest to how much I enjoy looking up at the stars on a clear evening. When I guided canoe trips during college in the North Woods of Maine, I longed for clear, summer nights on large lakes away from artificial light. The reach of the horizon and the extent of the nighttime sky were nothing short of incredible. Was this sense of wonder or fascination itself a marker or signpost of the divine? For now, though, I was trying to see if the existence of God could be deduced from available evidence—something that appeared more tangible and presumably, therefore, more reliable than some general concepts of awe and wonder.

Professor Hall reminded me that the cosmological argument is an *a posteriori* argument because, unlike *a priori* arguments, it relies on experience and observable reality. *A posteriori* essentially means "after experience." This started to make more sense. The principle of causality, also known as the principle of sufficient reason, requires that we find a cause for all things. Every effect must have a cause, and an infinite regress of causes (i.e., Who caused God?) is impossible. The buck needs to stop somewhere. We must have first cause. Why does the universe exist? Something, itself uncaused, caused it. And we call that something "god."

Atheists counter this argument in a variety of ways. Some insist that we just haven't yet discovered the natural first cause. Others say we have no reason for not having an infinite regress rather than a first cause. Still others suggest that the universe "is all there ever was and all there ever will be," as atheist and astronomer Carl Sagan famously put it.[3]

I had to acknowledge at least one of the atheists' points. Even if an initial cause is required, I didn't see any reason why that first cause must necessarily be the Christian God. This observation reminded me that, even as I tried to address this big question of existence, it might only get me part way there—a big part, probably a very big part, but the prudent course seemed to be to recognize that these classical arguments addressed only whether a god existed. Even if I became confident with that idea, to accept Christianity I would still have to make a connection (or leap) to Jesus Christ. But first things first.

By this time I was fully engaged and honestly curious and proceeded on to the classical argument about the cosmic watchmaker.

As a lawyer, I am almost always concerned with evidence. Looking at another *a posteriori* argument made a lot of sense to me. This one answers the question, "What do our observations and experiences in the natural world tell us about whether or not God exists?" It does that by appealing to the way we normally draw conclusions: we examine the evidence. For many, the world obviously exhibits design and purpose, taken as evidence for or signposts to God. Some Christians find confirmation of this idea in Scripture itself: "The heavens declare the glory of God; the skies proclaim the work of his hands" (Psalm 19:1).

Based upon the Greek word *telos* meaning, "end," "purpose," or "goal," this argument is known as the teleological argument. In short, it says that if the world was designed with an end in mind, for a purpose, a designer must exist, and that designer is God.

William Paley, an eighteenth-century British Christian apologist and philosopher, employed the teleological argument when he asked what conclusions a reasonable person would draw if he or she happened upon a pocket watch out in a field (actually, as a Brit, in a "heath"). Would he or she conclude that the watch was the product of pure chance? Or would the complexity and design of the watch point logically and necessarily to a watchmaker? Thus, if design exists in the world, a designer must exist, and that designer is God. The logic was sound. The premise I had to resolve was whether the world actually exhibited design.

Atheists and other detractors suggest that any apparent design is a function of evolutionary adaptations and not the product of a designer or an intelligent creator. In *The Blind Watchmaker*, accomplished British biologist, Richard Dawkins, argues that evolution is wholly capable of explaining not only the origin of life but also the complexity found in the world. For Dawkins then, he may see, at best, an "appearance" of design in the world but no *evidence* of design.

From what I understood, evolution seemed nearly impossible to refute or ignore. Scientists like Francis Collins accepted evolution. From my reading, I was unconvinced that evolution could explain the origin of life, but it otherwise seemed tenable that evolution might be responsible for the design and variety found in nature. Who was I to second-guess Dr. Collins? As I learned though, even if generally true, the next question was whether evolution was the sole explanation for what we observe in the world, or might it be the means by which an intelligent Creator accomplished the design observed in the natural world. Many Christians accept evolution. It is not an "either/or" proposition for them. I really wasn't sure where I came out on this topic, and the more I read, the more nuanced the issues appeared to be.

Later in my journey, I supplemented my analysis of the classical "design" or teleological argument by studying more modern writings that have attracted significant attention under the banner of "intelligent design" or simply ID. I discovered that biologists, evolutionists, and other scientists have been in a major brawl with Christian thinkers over Paley's watch and his hypothetical watchmaker. Proponents of ID point to what they call "irreducible complexity" in biological systems and other evidence of intelligence found throughout the world. Based on those observations, they posit God as the only reasonable source of that complexity and intelligence.

Richard Dawkins and other atheists argue that even if we allow for the theists' argument, the designer would have to be as complex, if not more intelligent and complex, than the universe he created. This, Dawkins concludes, makes the hypothesis of the designer just as improbable as the universe. To the extent that we need a source of intelligence, Dawkins falls back on an insistence that the theists still have to answer the question of who or what created the Creator. That sounded a lot like the unsatisfactory reply (the infinite regress) to the First Cause argument.

My reaction to Dawkins's position was fairly swift. I saw that the dog was chasing its tail. Dawkins's retort pointed not to any definitive answer but rather to an infinite regression. Aided by a series of podcasts by R.C. Sproul, I came to understand more clearly that Dawkins's reply was inconsistent with or ignored the very concept of God. By definition, as Sproul explained, God was self-existent and endowed with whatever the world required including whatever information and intelligence were required for life; that is, God did not require a creator. It wasn't that I now accepted design as conclusive evidence of God, but I did accept that if God existed, his nature as a self-existent being adequately responded to Dawkins's objection.

In contrast to Dawkins, another atheist, British philosopher Anthony Flew, announced in 2004 that he had rejected his lifelong disbelief in God. He acknowledged a "growing empathy with the insight of Einstein and other noted scientists that an Intelligence had to be behind the integrated complexity of the physical universe" and his "own insight that the integrated complexity of life itself—which is far more complex than the physical Universe—can only be explained in terms of an Intelligent Source."[4]

In addition to positing God as the author of evolution and the source of the intelligence found in the world, many thinkers including Dr. Francis Collins, who led the effort to map human DNA, express affinity for what has been called the anthropic principle. For me, the anthropic principle is closely related to and easily confused with other "design" arguments, like the modern intelligent design and the classical teleological arguments. Its name comes from the Greek word *anthropos* meaning "man" and focuses on the improbability that any location in the universe might permit human life to exist at all. Despite that improbability, however, life exists, thereby pointing to an omnipotence required to make such life possible on our earth.

Sometimes the anthropic principle is referred to as the "Goldilocks effect"—the world in which we live is "not too hot" and "not too cold" but "just right" to support human life. In their book *I Don't Have Enough Faith to Be an Atheist*, Norman Geisler and Frank Turek set out the enormous odds against life originating on earth without an intelligent creator. They write (note that the symbol ^ below means "to the power of"):

> *It's not that there are just a few broadly defined constants that may have resulted by chance. No, there are more than 100 very narrowly defined constants that strongly point to an intelligent Designer.*
>
> *Astrophysicist Hugh Ross has calculated the probability that these and other constants (122 in all) would exist today for any planet in*

the universe by chance (i.e., without Divine design). Assuming there are 10^{22} planets in the universe (a very large number: 1 with 22 zeros following it), his answer is shocking; one chance in 10^{138}, that's one chance in one with 138 zeros after it. There are only about 10^{70} atoms in the entire universe.

In effect, there is zero chance that any planet in the universe would have the life-supporting conditions we have, unless there is an intelligent Designer behind it all.[5]

Geisler and Turek then spell out fifteen anthropic constants that must be satisfied for life to exist as we know it. These include just enough gravitational force, the right carbon dioxide levels, and the universe's correct rate of expansion. Another scientist, the noted physicist Freeman Dyson, made one of the clearest expressions of this fine-tuning argument: "The more I examine the universe and the details of its architecture, the more I find that the universe in some sense must have known we were coming."[6] The focus of the anthropic argument thus is the emphasis that earth has been so precisely and uniquely constituted as to permit human life to exist that it "knew" that "we"—people—were coming.

The well-known astronomer, Fred Hoyle, earlier reached a similar conclusion:

A commonsense interpretation of the facts suggests that a super intellect has monkeyed with physics, as well as chemistry and biology, and that there are no blind forces worth speaking about in nature. The numbers one calculates from the facts seem to me so overwhelming as to put this conclusion almost beyond question.[7]

Or as astrophysicist Hugh Ross memorably put it, the likelihood of early cell life coming about by purely natural means is similar to the likelihood of a fully functional Boeing 747 being the natural result of a tornado racing through a junkyard.[8]

Like Geisler, Turek, Hoyle, and Ross, Francis Collins acknowledged that he was overwhelmed by the odds against life as we know it. Collins, who now heads the National Institute of

Health, summarizes his thoughts by commenting, "Our universe is wildly improbable."[9] He writes:

> *When you look from the perspective of a scientist at the universe, it looks as if it knew we were coming. There are 15 constants—gravitational constant, various constants about the strong and weak nuclear force, etc. that have precise values. If any one of those constants was off by even one part in a million, or in some cases, by one part in a million million, the universe could not have actually come to the point where we see it. Matter would not have been able to coalesce; there would have been no galaxy, stars, planets or people.*[10]

Although Collins acknowledges that future scientific investigation may shed some light on the enormous coincidence of physical factors permitting life to exist, he concludes, in a very understated manner, "The Anthropic Principle certainly provides an interesting argument in favor of a Creator.[11] Because of this great improbability, some formulate or restate the anthropic argument as the argument from statistical improbability. Improbable indeed. I began to think that the probability of my completing a marathon might actually be higher than the suggestion that all of life and all of the related complexity and intelligence in the world was the product of time and chance.

Just as they had humbled many scientists, the various design arguments fascinated me. Not only did they point to an intelligent Creator, but (other than a method for investigation) science had little to offer to explain the origin of biological life, the source of intelligence, the irreducible complexity in living things, the fine-tuning of the universe or the general appearance of design. For me, I guess, the jury was still out. Not being a scientist or trained to any degree in the rigors of scientific investigation, I remained—pardon the pun—agnostic as to whether design in nature convincingly established the existence of God.

Although the First Cause argument exhibited impeccable logic and has probably been the most obvious argument since man could stare at the night sky, it did not resonate in a way that it became motivational for me. The teleological, intelligent design, and anthropic arguments were not just fascinating, but held almost tangible appeal. At some level they were observable daily. Though these observations didn't end my inquiry in any way, they did sharpen my focus and enliven my resolve to continue, believing the journey might well be worthwhile. After all, if the Christian message was correct, the prize at the end of the trip was, as they say in the MasterCard commercial: priceless.

CHAPTER 5

THE RUN: MAKING PROGRESS (MTT)

The one thing I do know. I was blind but now I see.

— John 9:25 (NIV)

Ukrop's Monument Avenue 10K is run every year on either the last Saturday of March or the first one in April. As the event title indicates, the race is staged on Richmond's historic "Monument Avenue," which may be even more beautiful than historic.

The avenue is tree lined and has a wide grass median separating the flow of traffic. It was, they say, designed with Boston's Commonwealth Avenue in mind. On both sides of the street are elegant brick townhomes, most of them built in the early twentieth century. A Richmond website says that Monument Avenue is the only street in the United States that is a National Historic Landmark. At race time in the spring, the front gardens are alive with dazzling displays of bright flowers.

The race attracts a large group of participants—elite runners, college students, local joggers, and moms and dads with children out for a good walk. In recent years, more than 40,000 participants run, jog, trot, and walk the route, making it one of the largest races in the country.

Prize money is offered to the elite runners, who complete

the 10-kilometer (6.2 mile) circuit up Monument Avenue and back in around twenty-eight minutes. Monetary prizes are also awarded for the best costumes, so Elvis impersonators, Santa Claus, kayakers, characters from "Monty Python and the Holy Grail," living toilet paper rolls, and Sancho Panza on his donkey are running, too. Add cheerleading squads and bands along the route to encourage the runners, and it's a wonderful community event.

On race day I arrived at the starting area. I was *not* wearing a funny costume. If anything I was anxious and a bit too serious.

In the past, I had run the race haltingly with our older daughter, Brooke. I had also walked it with Cheryl and Amy. This year, however, would be different. After being fairly faithful to the Y training team schedule, I believed I could finish the race at my typical running pace, which, by that time, was about eleven minutes a mile—much improved from where I started.

Because of the large number of participants, the Monument Avenue 10K is run in "waves." Based upon a person's projected finish time, he or she is assigned a wave beginning with Wave A. Those who want to be in Waves A or B, with or even near the fastest runners, have to prove they belong by producing an official, fast time in another race. Race marshals try to police the various runners in the waves to prevent the congestion, collisions, and unnecessary chaos that occur when too many slow runners start ahead of fast runners. If someone wants to run with a friend, the two should run in the wave assigned to the slower runner. I found my way to my wave, K. Many blocks and many waves behind, Cheryl and Amy were preparing to start their own 10K odyssey with the walker group.

After the starting gun fired and Wave A zoomed away, the remaining waves were released at two- or three-minute intervals. As one wave left the start, the next would walk up to the line. This meant that the waves of runners and walkers stretched quite a long way back at race time. In fact about an hour and a half passes before the last wave, the walkers, arrives at the starting line to begin their 6.2-mile trek.

In order to give everyone an accurate finish time, each runner or walker ties a timing chip to his or her shoe, and a computer knows when each participant crosses both the starting and the finish lines, providing instant feedback on the morning's efforts.

As I joined my wave, I kept pretty much to myself. Not to be anti-social, but I had decided to run alone so I could focus on my pace. In the excitement of the moment surrounded by a crowd, a runner can get going too fast. I had come a long way even to be in the field of runners. The process was good for me, and now I wanted a good conclusion to this stage of my fitness journey. I might not be fast, but the one thing I knew was that I could finish this race. That is, I could finish the race if I kept in mind that transformational thought I had when I started running with the 10K Training Team: Find and then run at *your own pace*. I skipped my law firm's group photo to try to avoid getting around people who might, unwittingly, cause me to run faster than I should.

When our starting time came, I moved up to the line with the other four hundred people in Wave K. The starter shouted, "Go!" and off we went—shuffling, walking, trotting, and finally breaking into a run as the pack began to thin.

I had some nervous energy as we took off, but otherwise I felt pretty good. The race began on Broad Street and in few hundred yards turned left onto Lombardy Street. After that, as the statute of Confederate General J.E.B. Stuart loomed straight ahead, we turned right onto Monument Avenue, and thousands of runners became visible up ahead on the tree-lined avenue, all heading west.

After another few hundred yards we passed by one of Richmond's most famous landmarks, the statue of Robert E. Lee mounted on horseback in the middle of a prominent traffic circle. Remember, it is called "Monument" Avenue. Stuart and Lee are joined by Stonewall Jackson, Jefferson Davis, Matthew Maury, and Arthur Ashe—yes, African-American tennis star Arthur Ashe.

In the mid-1990s a citizen group organized to honor Ashe—a Richmond native and US Open tennis champion—with a statue in the city. Different sites were considered, but many were adamant that Ashe's statute be placed on Monument Avenue. Some believed this was inappropriate because it was inconsistent with the street's Confederate theme. Others thought it should be on Monument Avenue precisely because of the street's Confederate theme and the outdated reverence for a society that fought to preserve slavery.

The race route is essentially three miles up Monument Avenue, a U-turn, and three miles back down the same street on the other side of the median. Since the elite runners start earlier and run faster, we slower participants beginning our outbound leg saw them running toward us and headed for the finish with less than a mile to go. In admiration of how swift these elite runners are, many of the recreational runners (including me) took a moment to applaud and cheer as they ran by. With these preliminaries out of the way, I began to focus on the run.

Mile 1 marker (which is also approximately the spot for the Mile 5 marker): I checked the timing clock for my split time, did some math because of the staggered start, and found that I had completed the first mile in just over ten minutes, a fair bit faster than planned. As I had been told or warned, that's not unusual. The combination of excitement about the race, the effort to create some space around you, and the crowd of people often causes runners to head out quicker than they planned or expected.

Remembering one of the most common tips I heard—"Don't go out too fast at the start"—I consciously backed down my pace a bit. "Highways jammed with broken heroes on a last chance power drive," intoned one of Richmond's many garage bands as we ran by. Local cheerleading squads, sleepy Fan District residents, and many other race fans spread out along the route. "We are proud of you! We are proud of you! Keep it up!" they yelled. I was amazed and encouraged that they were still out there cheering for a bunch of plodders like me.

By the turnaround to head back downtown on the opposite side of the grass median, I was just a bit faster than my hoped for pace. Less than three miles to go; I felt very good and sensed a cautious, inward smile. I had settled into a good pace, and I was already thinking this wasn't going to be that hard after all.

We moved past the Confederate monuments and the Arthur Ashe statue again between miles four and five. Feeling good, I looked around and took in the street's large homes with their fascinating variety of architecture: Victorian, English Tudor, Colonial, Georgian, Spanish, Jacobean, Beaux Arts and Italianate. For a short stretch, the race participants run over century old cobblestones—always a challenge for runners.

I continued to focus on my pace. Nothing seemed to hurt, and, though I was getting tired, it was not serious. The route is very flat, having essentially no elevation changes, something for which I was grateful.

By the Mile 5 marker, I was still running well, that is, well for me. My pace remained steady and the wheels were not coming off. Sensing a good finish, I sped up just a little.

As I came down the final stretch to the finish line, the crowds got much deeper, and I heard an announcer call out the names of finishers as he picked out bib numbers and quickly looked up the names. Finally, I ran under the banner, across the finish line, and slowed to a walk. Volunteers removed the timing chip from my shoe, and I was done.

I had completed the 6.2-mile course in sixty-four minutes, just a little better than my expected—or hoped for—time of sixty-six minutes. I was pleased as I shuffled through a congested finishers' area. Volunteers handed out water, energy drinks, bagels, bananas, and more, while local singer-songwriter Susan Greenbaum prepared to perform.

I know I'm biased because Richmond is in my hometown, but the Ukrop's Monument Avenue 10K has got to be one of the world's great races. Even Bart Yasso of *Runner's World* fame considers the race to be one of his "Must-Do Races Near and Abroad." Here is what he said in his book, *My Life on the Run,* which was published the year after my run:

Runners of similar abilities start in waves of 1,000, fueling competitive spirits on a fast course. Bands play every quarter mile, upping the energy level of the runners. More than 25,000 people participate, and runners are grouped by a previous race's finish. Monument Avenue was named one of the country's 10 Great Streets by the American Planning Association. Six historic monuments are on the street including five that pay tribute to the Civil War and one to tennis player Arthur Ashe, a son of Richmond.[12]

So, I had completed a 10K race. I had lost almost thirty pounds as I trained. I was sleeping very well with the assistance of my CPAP machine. People began to remark how much better I looked—not just the weight loss, but my lack of fatigue. And, as mentioned earlier, some even suggested that my complexion had improved, noting that months earlier it reflected an unhealthy grayness. I had accomplished much, but I wanted to and needed to continue my pursuit of this new, improved lifestyle. I needed a plan to continue running. Fortunately, as I was beginning to learn, I had lots of opportunities.

When Randy and I ran that first marathon during college in 1978, the country was in the midst of what some have called the first running boom in the United States, which in large part was the result of Frank Shorter's success in the 1972 and 1976 Olympics (winning gold and silver), Bill Rogers' success in the Boston Marathon at the same time, and Steve Prefontaine's exciting racing style and victories. When we ran the Marine Corps Marathon later that year, more than three thousand had entered that race. That was considered a great field at the time, making it one of the two or three biggest races in the country. Today, the Marine Corps Marathon routinely sells out in a few weeks, capping its entrants at 30,000 runners. In fact, these initial years of the twenty-first century have witnessed such significant growth in running that we appear to be in a second running boom. From 5K and 10K races to marathons and even longer events, running has never been more popular.

The first New York City Marathon, in 1970, had only one hundred twenty runners. In 2006, so many were interested that it was capped at 38,000. To run this marathon, individuals have to either run a qualifying time in another marathon or participate in the entrance lottery. Many other marathons sport fields of 30,000-40,000. Recently, Chicago began limiting its marathon to 40,000 who sign up first come, first served. The fabled Boston Marathon remains (for the most part) the only race where the *only* way to get a bib is to run a qualifying time in another marathon. All of which means that, with the exception of Boston, the diligent and the patient can run in nearly all the other major running events.

Let me add, however, that Boston and other races reserve some bibs for charity runners—people using the race as a vehicle to raise money for a specific charity. This combination of charitable fundraising and footraces has become big business. In a recent Chicago Marathon, for example, more than 9,500 charity runners raised money for more than 150 charities. Contributions were expected to exceed $10 million in just that one event.[13] This phenomenon extends beyond the United States. According to the Canadian Breast Cancer Foundation, the 2010 CIBC Run for the Cure raised $33 million.[14]

By 2009 the United States sported more than 17,000 road races with more than ten million individual finishers—up from fewer than four million just ten years earlier.[15] And I was now part of those statistics. I wanted to keep up the running and racing. Creating specific goals would help me do that. Could I build to longer distances and maybe even get up to 26.2 miles?

More important, could I keep up the discipline of weekly runs without a training team holding me accountable? I did not think so. I needed the positive peer pressure and encouragement. Convinced that I needed the structure and support of a training team along with the guidance of a training program and in spite of my misgivings, I signed up for the Richmond Sports Backer's Marathon Training Team or MTT as seen on oval stickers on rear windows and bumpers of runners' cars.

When I signed up for the MTT, I fully expected that as the long, Saturday runs increased to ten or twelve miles, I would have to check out. At least for a number of weeks, however, I would have a place I needed to be and a group with whom to run on Saturday mornings. That would motivate me through the week.

The day the first team meeting arrived, I drove the fifteen or twenty minutes to Sports Backer Stadium with doubts. Marathon training seemed like a good idea at sign-up time, but what business did I have signing up for an MTT? I felt intimidated that first Saturday morning. Believing that participating in 10K training could help me run 6.2 miles was one thing. A marathon was a completely different beast.

As I neared the stadium where our MTT would meet every Saturday morning, the traffic became unusually congested. As I turned the corner and could see the stadium, I discovered that the traffic jam was *there*. More than 880 signed up for the Richmond Sports Backer's Marathon Training Team.

Resisting the temptation to drive right by, I parked and took a closer look. Not every person was lean, long-legged, and tightly muscled. I saw a lot of normal looking people—people like me. Maybe I could get ready and complete the Richmond Marathon in five months. I had been able to build my training runs up to four or five miles and had run a 10K, but it wasn't easy. How, I wondered, could I take my longest distance, the 10K, and run it four times without stopping? More than that, I knew that my personal discipline was poor. How else did I get in such bad physical shape to begin with?

Signing up with a friend would have made the process easier, but there I was, by myself—at least for a few minutes. I stood with hundreds of individual runners with not a single team or group. Based upon the information on my MMT application, I was placed on the Orange team, the one for novices. I began to see some friendly faces including Val, a teacher from our girls' school who had already run a number of marathons using the run-walk method. I also saw Mary, a school parent friend who had the same objectives as I did and who faced some of the same challenges. Val, Mary, and others I would meet would prove to be a great source of inspiration and encouragement as training progressed.

Maybe—just maybe—I could run a marathon the year I turned fifty. If I were to do so, the next step would be hard, very hard. Despite these thoughts I also couldn't help but think (dream?) that if I were able to run a marathon, running in New York City would be very cool. And so, although I didn't tell a soul, I had applied for admission into the New York City Marathon, which was scheduled one week prior to Richmond.

Before long, I realized that I had less than five months to the starting gun for a much longer race, and time was counting down.

CHAPTER 6

THE RACE: TRUE FOR ME?

I had as many doubts as anyone else.
Standing on the starting line, we're all cowards.

—Alberto Salazar

In an odd way, my thinking about life and God took on the pattern of my running. Each step of the way encouraged me to accept the challenge of the next. And so, having been engaged by the logic of the First Cause argument and intrigued by the idea of intelligent design, I pressed on just as I had from my first run to dreams of a marathon. In both cases, as I went along, I found new vigor. Somewhere along the process I realized that I had already committed to a thorough review of the various "arguments" for God. If I was going to take the trouble of thinking through what I believed and why I believed it, I wanted to be as comprehensive as possible.

I noticed that an examination of the classic arguments required the consideration and use of sophisticated jargon like "ontological" and "anthropic" and Latin phrases like *a priori* and *a posteriori*. In a similar way, running offered more than a little of its own special words and technical jargon. *Runner's World* captured this well in one of its website articles, where it offered:

> *Anyone who has been running for a few years, and in particular trying to improve his or her marathon time, knows that training theory*

can get quite complex. You've got pace, you've got pulse, you've got
max VO2, you've got lactate threshold, you've got cruise intervals,
you've got tempo training, you've got enough gibberish to launch a
new line of dictionaries.[16]

In considering the evidence and arguments for God, I had,
in many ways, just scratched the surface, just as I had with my
running schedule. Yet, I continued to move forward in a fairly
systematic way. When I saw different articles and various lists that
featured twenty-five or thirty-six arguments for the existence
of God, I wondered if I could ever finish. The task might have
been as daunting as running twenty-six miles, but I pressed
on—surprisingly not discouraged, but invigorated. That said,
I realized I would likely need more than optimism and vigor to
run the marathon. And, at this time, if I were a betting man, I
still would assume that I'd never complete a run of that length.

Speaking of gambling, the next of the classic arguments
concerning God that I considered is known as Pascal's Wager—
developed by the seventeenth century French mathematician and
philosopher Blaise Pascal. Again, I seemed transported to Rogers
Hall at William & Mary to be reminded of what is sometimes
called a "pragmatic" argument for believing in God.

As a practical matter, this argument or "wager" posits that it is
far better to believe in God and be wrong than to reject belief in
God and be wrong. More specifically, if we believe in God, and God
actually exists, we receive and enjoy the benefits of that belief
such as forgiveness and eternal life. If we believe in God and it
turns out we are wrong, and God does not exist, we experience
no bad consequences. Conversely, if we decide not to believe in
God and it turns out that God exists, the consequences appear
to be dire: judgment, rejection, and eternal damnation. Simply
put, if you are a betting person, you would be better off to bet
on God. I recall one of my freshman hall mates, also enrolled
in Philosophy 101, found this particularly appealing. I wasn't so
sure. Something didn't seem right.

While Pascal's Wager has a certain logic, it seemed more like a word game than an intellectually satisfying argument, even less so than the Ontological Argument. To my way of thinking, a statement or an idea must have a level of sincerity before it can legitimately be called a belief. Faith must be more than merely stating the words, "This I believe." And if an omniscient God exists, he knows what is in our hearts, and no real belief is in our hearts if we simply adopt Pascal's Wager. To me, Pascal's approach seemed like cheating or faking it. Making a bet seemed worse in many ways than refusing to believe. If someone is merely "betting" on God, and God exists, such insincerity and lack of integrity would more likely be worse in degree than any hoped for benefits. So Pascal's Wager was not a bet I intended to place. Too much was at stake to resolve the question with a gamble. I wanted to know if a clearer and more certain answer was discernible.

Having said that, and although I expressly rejected Pascal's Wager, if I believed the things I was saying about God, salvation, and the Church, why wasn't I living my life differently, better? Why didn't my everyday actions better reflect the life-changing qualities of Christian faith? I realized that I nonetheless appeared to be living my life as if Pascal's Wager *was* the basis for whatever beliefs I held or whatever faith I practiced. That was an unsettling thought. If I did not believe those things I recited in the Apostles' Creed, why was I doing it? And, if I was affirming belief every week by making significant statements that I did not believe, what kind of person was I? At a minimum, as I had seen in Arnold Palmer, I had to preserve some fundamental integrity. I needed to be in or out. For that I needed to have answers.

This process was beginning to feel like signing up for the MTT. I pressed on in my training with increased desire, interest, and anxiety about the race to come. I pressed on with my study of the arguments for the existence of God with the same desire, interest, and anxiety. While one may appreciate the potential anxiety related to completing a long run, the anxiety relating to a journey of faith may be less intuitive; I had now put myself in a position (I needed to be in or out) where either choice surfaced consequences I did not think I was prepared to handle. Yet, I was on a road, and I wanted to and needed to press on.

Many philosophers, theists, and Christians find support for the validity of a transcendent God in the existence of objective moral truth—in the belief that there is a difference between right and wrong, that we can know the difference, and that, in fact, we *do* know the difference. I recalled reading years earlier a particularly compelling presentation by C.S. Lewis on this topic in *Mere Christianity* where he writes about the "Law of Human Nature." I decided to find and reread that book. I also recalled now that both Zacharias and Keller had talked in sermons or podcasts about the "moral lawgiver" or "moral" argument. So, I turned my focus to that classic argument.

Initially I understood that argument in this simple way: if a moral law exists, so must a lawgiver. This seemed fairly straightforward and logical. The more I studied, however, the more I began to realize that our sense of right and wrong, longing for justice, and conscience have different layers, forms, and nuances, but they all appeared to point to the existence of a supreme being.

I considered the traditional moral lawgiver argument as proof of God's existence. This approach begins with the proposition that objective moral truth exists and then argues back to the approach that no objective moral truths or absolutes exist.

A related formulation of the moral argument is that God is necessary because there must be a final or ultimate arbiter of right and wrong; someone who determines right from wrong on a final basis. As I explored this line of thinking, I read the explanation by R.C. Sproul of the nuance beyond the simple "lawgiver" argument. Specifically, recalling Immanuel Kant's take on these issues of morality and a transcendent source, Sproul explained that any ethical or moral judgment only makes sense in a world with justice, and justice in turn requires that we must have ultimate consequences for our conduct; and the only source for such ultimate justice is a judge, who, of course, is God.

To respond to these arguments, I had to examine whether I believed that we can draw any conclusions about human behavior and ethical conduct that are objectively true—true without regard to the moment, the society, or any particular circumstances. Moreover, if I accepted that such moral truths exist, I needed to examine whether I should then conclude that the only source for such absolutes is God. The ethical relativist rejects truth and so has no problem walking away from any debate about the existence of God premised on moral absolutes. That person doesn't believe any exist. This required me to face the widely held, modern belief that all questions of right and wrong are relative, that ethical conduct varies depending upon the different belief systems of individuals and/or societies—that questions of right and wrong are relative.

In contemporary culture, many individuals and commentators believe that right or wrong are relative. In fact, a major tenant of these "post-modern"[17] times appears to be that everyone can create his or her own truth. Thus many people today do not believe that objective moral truth exists. They do not believe that certain things are simply, clearly, and irrefutably right or wrong in all places and at all times. Rather, they subscribe to the belief that what may be right for some may not be right for others and that no one has the right to suggest that one person's beliefs are right and another's are wrong. ("I'm okay; you're okay.")

But the cry of the relativist was not resonating with me. Both logically and viscerally, it did not appear to make sense. This struck me more intensely one day as I listened to The Teaching Company course, "Books that Have Made History: Books that Can Change Your Life" with Professor J. Rufus Fears from the University of Oklahoma. In summarizing the themes in the biblical Book of Job, Fears asked: "Can we determine if things that happen to us are absolutely bad or absolutely good or is it just a matter of circumstances?" He then went on to say:

> . . . [A]s a nation we have made the decision that there is no such thing as absolute good or absolute evil—it simply depends upon the

circumstances; and those are perfectly reasonable conclusions to reach as individuals and as a nation.[18]

If Professor Fears is right, then no moral absolutes exist, and the moral argument fails before it gets started. But I wondered how this professor could make such a statement. When did our nation come to the "perfectly reasonable conclusion" that everything is relative? Was that question a proposition on the ballot during the last election cycle, and I just missed it? The more I thought about this conclusion, the more I was troubled. In addition, as logicians point out, proponents of relativism have a difficult time sustaining their rejection of absolute truth claims on a philosophical level because to state, "No absolutes exist," is itself an absolute. The relativist's claim is a contradiction; it refutes itself. Perhaps more importantly, relativism did not square with how I encountered life itself.

As superficially attractive and tolerant as relativism appears, upon close inspection, such a view of human interaction didn't square with my own thoughts, feelings, and experiences. I harkened back to something C.S. Lewis said—that not only does a moral law exist, but that every person *knows* such a law exists. That's what I seemed to conclude whenever I really thought about it.

Listening to Tim Keller one morning during a four-mile run helped me better understand this sense I had about objective morality. Keller commented that his own thinking about relativism had been influenced by a law review article written by Yale Law School professor Arthur Leff. After replaying Keller's sermon a number of times so I could catch the author's name and date of publication, I found and read Leff's article, "Unspeakable Ethics, Unnatural Law," published in the *Duke Law Journal.*[19] As Keller indicated, Leff made a powerful presentation exposing both the perils of moral relativism and the human recognition that we *know* that certain things are clearly right and wrong.

Although an agnostic, Leff suggested that we cannot have an objective moral truth without God. Specifically, Leff makes the compelling case that human beings, left to their own intellect and ingenuity, cannot establish immutable ethical principles for living. He explained that for humans, "There is no way to prove one ethical or legal system superior to any other, unless at some point an evaluator is asserted to have the final, uncontradicted, unexamined word. That choice of unjudged judge, whoever is given the role, is itself, strictly speaking, arbitrary."[20]

Keller explained that any system of morality based upon human constructs requires the assertion of power by someone who determines what is right or wrong. As Leff puts it, the question, "Sez who?" must be answered. Absent an unjudged judge or divine arbitrator, any determination of right and wrong results from the assertion of power by either a majority or a despot. After an interesting discussion of various issues about ethics and lawmaking, including a survey of each possible paradigm, Leff closes his essay with the following:

> *All I can say is this: it looks as if we are all we have. Given what we know about ourselves and each other, this is an extraordinarily unappetizing prospect; looking around the world, it appears that if all men are brothers, the ruling model is Cain and Abel. Neither reason, nor love, nor even terror, seems to have worked to make us "good," and worse than that, there is no reason why anything should. Only if ethics were something unspeakable by us, could law be unnatural, and therefore unchallengeable. As things now stand, everything is up for grabs:*
> *Nevertheless:*
> *Napalming babies is bad.*
> *Starving the poor is wicked.*
> *Buying and selling each other is depraved.*
> *Those who stood up to and died resisting Hitler, Stalin, Amin, and Pol Pot—and General Custer too—have earned salvation.*
> *Those who acquiesced deserve to be damned.*
> *There is in the world such thing as evil.*
> *[All together now:] Sez who?*
> *God help us.*[21]

Leff was able to both demonstrate and articulate persuasively the very thing I had sensed. Some things just appear to be true or correct—universally and undeniably so, particularly in the area of right and wrong. This seemed to be universal and undeniable. Even he appears to acknowledge that despite his own doubts, some objective moral truths nonetheless exist.

As Kant, Leff, and Keller had all explained, if no God exists, then we have no final arbiter of right and wrong. Without God, we have no basis to claim that one person's belief or action is any more correct or moral than another person's different or opposite belief or action. The only basis then would be to impose a standard with force—with power, which is what Leff meant when he posed the schoolyard taunt: "Sez who?"

I believed—*I knew*—that certain things were right and certain things were wrong without regard for my opinion, another's opinion, or society's opinion. Torturing babies is wrong, as is starving the poor or forcing individuals into prostitution. The essential veracity of these conclusions, to me, was self-evident in the sense that our founding fathers saw the right to "life, liberty, and the pursuit of happiness" to be self-evident. They not only resonated deep within me, but called for action to establish good and combat evil.

I could now see plainly that the recognition of universal moral truth led very logically to the moral arguments. Yet, not only did these arguments make sense rationally, they had what Ravi Zacharias called experiential relevance. They made sense with the way we encounter the world and life every day. They made sense outside of a philosopher's workshop. The Ontological Argument, for instance, did not affect my day-to-day thinking and doing. Not only did the sense of right and wrong resonate, but something N.T. Wright referred to as a "longing for justice" resonated as well. Thus, not only did I believe in right and wrong being accessible objectively, but I also sensed a desire and a need for some form of justice—that wrongs would be righted in some ultimate sense. If this moral sense was not only strong, but affected everyday behavior, what might be its source?

Who determines which beliefs are correct? Absent a perfectly just judge's final word, all we have are competing truth claims waiting for the strong to impose their truth claims on the weak.

With that, the moral argument began to resonate powerfully with me largely because I accepted the argument's starting point and fundamental tenant, that absolute, objective moral truths are real. Thus, I began to acknowledge more openly that some things are always right or always wrong. In fact, I could (and can) say confidently that I *do* believe that moral truths exists that should serve as the bedrock of personal conduct for all human interaction. Moreover, this belief has a certainty that is distinctly more meaningful than simply a logical "proof" or a rational conclusion. It has a vibrant, current life and meaning that matched my experience and mattered on a day-to-day basis.

Who then would want to argue that Leff's observations are wrong? Like C. S. Lewis observed, we know these moral truths so well that we not only recoil at the thought of things like torture or genocide, but, if faced with such things, we would be moved to take action. To revisit the starting point, then, I refocused by asking what this conclusion told me about the existence of God. What about Leff's observations provides insight into the question about the existence of God?

Classic theorists of the moral argument explain that the source of an absolute moral law must be a lawgiver and that the lawgiver must be God because a moral order requires a transcendent source. As Leff so eloquently had demonstrated, any source of a moral law other than a transcendent source, such as the consensus of human society (sometimes referred to as the "skeptic's choice") is subject to change as a result of changes in the human condition, changes in human institutions, or even changes in human intellectual fads. We certainly all know of behaviors that were considered wrong, if not illegal, in the past that are now permitted. To be a moral absolute, it must be true at all times and with all people.

Murder must be wrong in Nazi Germany as well as in 21st century America. Likewise, racism must be wrong in nineteenth-century South Africa as well as twenty-first-century China. Thus the source of the moral law must be external to man so that it can be eternal and immutable. Furthermore, for a moral absolute to be undeniable it must be perfect and unchanging. Only an eternal and faultless God could establish such laws and justice. The modern Christian philosopher and Bishop of Durham, N.T. Wright, looks to the human longing for justice as one of the essential "echoes of a voice" that are signposts to God.[22] I agreed.

The acceptance of moral truths and the desire for justice certainly appeared to point to God. Although I had no other answer and did not find any skeptics with a reasoned solution, just as I continued to question whether I could complete the marathon, I continued to question and doubt—but perhaps some things were becoming more certain.

Just as my fitness had improved—I could run much longer distances now—I agreed with Immanuel Kant's observation that there were two things we cannot ignore: "the starry skies above and the moral law within." While the first cause argument ("the starry skies above") had impeccable logic, the moral lawgiver argument ("the moral law within") appealed to my more intuitive side. Like adding distance gradually in my running, I was growing in my understanding of the philosophical basis for a belief in God. For my purposes, I was making real progress.

Affinity for the moral argument helped to move me measurably along my journey. And while it may not have convinced me irrefutably, I was eager to understand more. Could I find some further confirmation? In the vernacular of my profession, I needed to research the case law and determine whether my initial findings were supported by the weight of authority. I had to make sure there were not any strong, persuasive decisions that objective morals did not exist.

In plain language, just as I needed to keep running for my physical health, apparently I needed to keep thinking for my spiritual health. I found more books to read, I had more podcasts to listen to, and I had a new milestone, a "half-marathon" to run.

CHAPTER 7

THE RUN: BECOMING A RUNNER

But those that hope in the Lord shall renew their strength;
they shall mount up with wings as eagles;
they shall run, and be not weary;
they shall walk, and not faint.

—Isaiah 40:31 (KJV)

For my first week at the Richmond Sports Backers Marathon Training Team or MTT, the group run was only three miles. I went out very fast and finished before most others but without any issues. I came back for week two, which was four miles—so far, so good. I began to meet some of my fellow novice runners and realized that many, if not most, were as new and as intimidated as I was. The team's coaches and the other team members were all incredibly supportive. No one cared about time. Everyone cared about each other.

Not only had I finished the 10K, but now I had the audacity to sign up for a marathon training team. The good news was that I was sticking to it. Like the 10K Training Team, the MTT had a recommended weekly schedule of runs that, if followed, should prepare a person for the big day and its 26.2 miles. The schedule for novice runners like me consisted of runs on Tuesday, Wednesday, and Thursday and a long run on every Saturday. So far, I had kept up with the schedule.

Just as the fact that I really knew about my professed faith was disturbing, the fact that I knew so little about running was comical. Four weeks into the program, we finished a five-mile run on a hot and humid July morning. As I came in and picked up a cup of water, one of our Orange team captains looked at my sweat soaked cotton shorts and T-shirt and suggested, "You might want to look into some of this dri-fit clothing, especially for these hot summer runs." So I went to our local running store and spoke to the sales personnel. After trying on a variety of shorts and shirts, I brought two pairs of running shorts and three shirts—all made of this "new" wicking fabric—essentially the same polyester that came in and went out of fashion as fast as disco and leisure suits during my college years in the late 1970s.

My new running shorts had a liner like a bathing suit, so when I got them home—as further evidence of my running naïveté—I wasn't sure if I was supposed to wear them with or without an undergarment. Apparently sensing this lack of basic information about running, as I made that first purchase at Richmond Road Runners, I walked around the store to take in some of the other equipment and accessories in this new sport I was beginning to adopt. I picked up the most recent edition of *Runner's World* and added it to my checkout items. This would lead to a subscription and another glimpse into the wider world of running. The magazine would be a source of great inspiration and good information but some frustration as well. For the novice runner, it had few tips more helpful than to get yourself to your local running store to speak with other runners who can help you with shoe fitting and a variety of other needs. And as much as I enjoy large chain stores like Dick's Sporting Goods, the local running store is almost certainly owned and staffed by members of the running community who, when not competing, are setting up the local races and making much of what happens for runners happen.

Shortly after I was equipped with my new dri-fit shorts and running shirts, we ran six miles on a warm Saturday morning. As I finished the run and turned into our meeting area near Sports

Backers Stadium, one of my coaches pointed out that blood appeared to be running down the front of my shirt—my new, *white* Nike dri-fit T-shirt. "Be careful to protect your nipples," he said. If I didn't appreciate what he meant at the time, about 30 or 45 minutes later in my shower, his advice was brought home stingingly clear. Alas, another revelation about running. While it seems self-evident now, the constant up and down movement of a running shirt (while not necessarily obvious) rubs across the chest. Yet, as runs get longer, the constant rubbing, while subtle, can do some unanticipated damage. Few need to be reminded more than once. For long runs, some runners use a product called Glide for protection, others (like me) tape Band-Aids over each nipple to avoid bloodied T-shirts and shocks to my nervous system when taking post-run showers.

Just as I had begun to devour numerous books, podcasts, and other materials to assist me in my journey of faith, in an effort to combat my naïveté about things running, I stopped by the library and picked up some books on the topic. Many are available, mostly written by former elite runners such as Bill Rogers, Hal Higdon, and Jeff Galloway. For the most part, the content and advice were similar. Sometimes the tone or approach of a particular author would show a bias for, or a greater focus on, experienced runners. In fact, advice for the truly new and novice runner was sometimes lacking. Perhaps most telling were comments like the following, which showed little concern for the novice or merely exposed the writers' arrogance. In discussing the new trend of LSD ("long, slow distance" running) and the increased novice participation in marathons, one writer commented, "I could not imagine being on my feet for more than three hours." Of course, most of us novice runners were looking at four or five hours or even longer to complete our first marathon.

After looking many other places, I found that the training guide provided by Sports Backers was an excellent compilation of the best and most relevant information—and it was written to be useful for novices, like me. Sometimes we ignore what is right in front of us, particularly if it is not packaged properly or wrapped in sophistication.

A few weeks into the MTT program, things seemed to be going well. Then, the time came for a new milestone for me—seven miles. Maybe not quickly, but after three or four weeks I had been able to cover the distance each Saturday. I was maintaining the daily run schedule; and because I had completed the 10K (6.2 miles), I thought I could probably conquer the week's mileage even though it was farther than I had gone in over twenty years.

I was meeting some other runners on the MTT, but still mostly running alone, broken by brief conversations with others—people my family likes to call "little while" friends. At this time, I preferred running alone. I wasn't sure I belonged on this marathon journey, and, in part due to this lack of confidence, I really wanted to make sure to run my own pace and not go so fast that I could not finish a particular day's distance. I also liked the contemplative time running alone not only offered but seemed to inspire.

As our group began the seven-miler and headed off toward Bryan Park, I was toward the head of the pack. I did not know at the time, but I had put myself in the middle of a pack of intermediate runners. Despite the high humidity at 7 A.M., I felt quite good. We ran up through some North Side neighborhoods and into the park. Then I started to fade. At about four miles into the run, I sensed things were not going as well, and I was slowing down. A guy and girl ran alongside and struck up a conversation, so I began to run with them. The camaraderie helped carry me along. I was tiring, but my "little while" runner friends helped make the rest of my run enjoyable, at least until we were within sight of the stadium and the finish to a milestone day. By that time, I could barely keep moving. I bid my friends to go on, slowed my pace, and determined to finish without walking in. I got through the final half mile after much hard work. I had another run under my belt—another milestone—but, I reminded myself, it was only seven miles, and it hadn't come easily. How would I ever complete 26.2 miles? And was I going to resolve the questions and doubts about my faith? I returned my focus to thinking about whether I knew of one thing I could accept with confidence.

After mid-week runs of three, five, and three miles, I was back the following Saturday. The group run that morning was, of course, eight miles and another milestone. I saw Dan—my new "little while" friend from the last week—in the parking lot as our group got ready for the day's run. Eight miles! That was a lot to me. Dan must have read my mind, as he said to our informal, assembled group—"Eight miles, just one more than last week. No problem." We greeted each other, spoke for a few moments, and then headed off together for that morning's run.

Who would have known that, with this run, without any spoken agreement or recognition, Dan would become my "running buddy"? We were about the same age, and we found that we ran at about the same pace; so we started looking for each other and running together each Saturday. And who would have predicted that even after the MTT we would meet for the next two years and head out for a long run each Saturday morning? The run that week seemed to go much better than just a week earlier. In fact, with less than a half a mile to go and the finish in sight, I picked up the pace and led Dan back home in what seemed to me to be a sprint. Winded, I nonetheless felt great. Some days are just better than others. Little by little the advice that our Training Guide and our coaches were giving was proving to be correct. Also, nothing is much better than catching up with a running buddy and helping to push each other along.

Almost every running program and advice book about distance running says that nothing can substitute for having a running buddy (or, better yet, running buddies). This new friend or "buddy" not only helps to get you to the start line each Saturday because someone is expecting you, but you look forward to the challenge and camaraderie *together*. One thing I know is that I could not have made it without Dan. For over five hundred miles we served as each other's "book on tape." During the next few months, Dan and I would hit the streets together, even when not part of the training team schedule. This never would have worked if we had not run at the same pace, but we had. And almost immediately we became very comfortable with each other and used large portions of our runs to discuss personal issues, work, family problems, mid-life opportunities as well as solving the world's problems.

As the Saturday MTT runs quickly went from three to five to seven miles and even more, we received e-mails telling us the route for upcoming Saturday, including the number and location of the "SAGs." A SAG would have water or Gatorade (and sometimes pretzels, gummy bears, and even energy gels). These SAGs were typically spaced every three or so miles and were not just welcome, but sorely needed. I am pretty sure I always stopped at a SAG and enjoyed some water or Gatorade.

At some point, after a number of fairly long, Saturday runs, I wondered what SAG stood for. Being a running neophyte, however, I was embarrassed to ask. It was obviously an acronym for something, but I couldn't figure out what. Finally, I dared to ask my new running buddy Dan. He didn't know either. So at the end of that day's run, we asked our team captain. When he didn't know either, suddenly, I didn't feel so bad not knowing, or asking.

Many times, I have observed, we are better off not knowing certain things. If my mother and my brother knew how many Civil War plaques, monuments, and historical markers my father and I were going to read at Gettysburg, they may have signed up for a different vacation stop. In a similar, but more sobering vein, imagine trying to recruit volunteers to land on the beaches of Normandy or hold the line in the Ardennes if everyone knew what the future held. This became particularly true as I began to learn about the strong mental aspect of distance running.

The more I committed myself to this new running crowd, the more I learned from new friends, coaches, and *Runner's World* how critical the mental aspect of running was. Dreaming about actually completing a marathon, I ran across comments like "The marathon is really two races—the first twenty, which is physical and the last six, which is all mental." I would need a twenty-six-mile run to learn some of the mind-body connections when nearing the finish.

In addition to group runs on Saturday, another new running friend organized a longish mid-week run. So Dan and I started meeting this informal group that organized itself at the Downtown YMCA. One week we planned to run eight miles. To get these longer runs done before work on Wednesdays, we would start around 5:15 A.M. Not surprisingly, we ran through Richmond's Fan District in the dark.

One early morning, as the group headed off, Dan and I fell in a little behind three women who often ran a pace similar to ours. Because of the darkness, the women missed a turn, and we followed. Soon we realized that, because of the mistake, we were likely going to run ten or eleven miles instead of the eight that had been planned. For me, this was surprisingly difficult. I could do the distance physically—by then I had run that distance a number of times—but I experienced the relationship between what I had prepared for mentally and what I now had to do physically. As a result of this disconnect, I struggled to finish those two extra miles. This and similar situations emphasized to me how critical mental preparation is for running long distances. If we were scheduled to run seven miles, when I finished I was tired and not sure I could have done eight or more that day. And the same was true of twelve and fourteen miles. I always finished tired and happy, but unsure I could have gone farther that day.

Training the mind for different running challenges was also brought home to me when the heat and the humidity went up as our MTT program continued. When I started running, everything was all new to me. The MTT had begun in June, a warm, but pleasant time to be in Richmond, Virginia. As we increased mileage and ran three and then five and then seven miles, the temperature rose. By July and August we were often running in 80-degree weather with 80-percent humidity—at 7 A.M.! But that was all I knew, so I persevered. I would finish a ten-mile run completely soaked in sweat, and sometimes my shoes would be soggy as the perspiration had rolled down my legs over the miles.

The challenge of running in the summer in Richmond is significant, a factor the MTT attempted to address by pushing our group's long-run start time back thirty minutes, such that we would start at 6:30 A.M. instead of 7:00 on Saturdays between July 4 and Labor Day, when we returned to the 7 A.M. start. When the time came, I would learn that just as I was conditioning my legs to carry me longer and longer distances, I had also been conditioning my mind for those long distances.

Sometimes, however, we never seem to learn. Or is that we just ignore that which we know to be true? Shortly after I converted from cotton to polyester for my running attire, I wore a sleeveless running shirt the law firm had given everyone who would be running in the Monument Avenue 10k. So, one week I wore this new shirt as Dan and I attempted to resolve many of the world's problems during a regular, long Saturday run. Sleeveless shirts have never been my style, but the day was hot, I was a new runner, and maybe this would be fine. I finished up a hot, but satisfying nine-mile jog with Dan—and, as was becoming our fashion— we each slipped on a clean, cotton T-shirt, said goodbye, and headed home. When I stepped into the shower, apparently not having learned the lesson of my bleeding nipples problem, I got a shockingly rude jolt as the water struck my triceps. I hadn't noticed that the edge of the sleeveless shirt fell against the back of my upper arms such that during nine miles on the roads a regular rubbing had removed some of the epidermis. Like a trained debater or persistent examiner, the shower water sought out the areas where I was most vulnerable.

Like my education about running, my grasp of the classical arguments relating to God's existence continued to grow. The two areas—running and faith—appeared more and more to intersect regularly. My running buddy Dan had some challenges at home with his children, and we used long Saturday runs to work through those and other personal issues. Dan, a Catholic Christian, mentioned how some of these issues had led him back to Mass, which opened the forum for a broader discussion of issues of faith.

We spent so much time on the streets together talking that Dan introduced hand signals for us to indicate to the other if the story one of us was starting to tell was the first, second, or third time the story had been told. Sometime later, during a particularly long run—probably fourteen or sixteen miles—I mentioned a particular case; and when I realized it was a new topic for him, I said, "Oh, this story will be good for six or seven miles." And it was. The next week Dan mentioned to another fellow runner as we set off that running with me was like his own book on tape. It should go without saying, that many of the thoughts in this book were vetted with Dan on the downtown streets of Richmond.

One day early in my running journey, I came home from work just after dusk. As I turned a corner in our neighborhood, which had no streetlights, I came dangerously close to a couple walking their dog. They were on the side of the street, and I was neither going too fast nor driving outside the middle of the fairly narrow road. It startled and scared me and made me see that—although I saw very few vehicles—the drivers couldn't see me most winter mornings. I realized cars that came uncomfortably close to me probably did so because the drivers could not see me until they were right upon me. Most runners will not fare well in a collision with a motorized vehicle. Our mothers were right: it's better to be safe....

So I stopped by our local running store and, though it challenged my manhood and undermined the cool factor, I purchased a neon yellow vest to wear when running in the dark. Unfortunately in keeping with my comical approach to running gear and learning the ropes, I had purchased a woman's vest and had to embarrassingly return it for the right one a few days later. Obviously, I had lots to learn in trying to become a runner.

One of the other time-tested rules of running I learned was not to go out too fast—particularly in races. That humid morning when I first met Dan and almost did not finish the seven-mile run, I later learned that the intermediate group had started with my beginner group, so I unwittingly had run an intermediate-type pace for two or three miles. The pace had been too fast, and

I had faded and almost crashed. As noted in my earliest days of running, finding one's own pace is vital.

Likewise, I had to avoid treating training runs as races. I had to prevent my ego from insisting that I finish in the lead pack. One of my law partners says he can't stand for anyone to pass him when he's out for a run. That attitude has created lots of problems for him when he tries to run in Central Park where every type of runner, including elites may be there any given morning. For me, then, I had to recognize right away that success could not be measured by what place I was when I finished any given run.

Most importantly, I was finding time to run regularly. I had made running part of my committed schedule. Some might think that I had discovered the joy of a good run and I couldn't wait each morning to get out there again. Many runners feel that way. You hear about the runner's high and read about the drug-like impact of endorphins. This was not and is not me. Many days are like that—simply a joy, if not exhilarating. But other days I find getting out there tough. I wish I had the urge to go for another run half as much as I have an urge to eat a donut or two if someone leaves a dozen within walking distance of my office at work. For me, that means I have to fight the temptation to take too many days off. Don't get me wrong; I can barely recall a single time when I didn't feel better when I had finished a run. I was almost always refreshed, energized, and just more "alive", to tackle the day. (Some often observe with only a trace of humor that most people also feel better when a session of torture ceases.)

While I may not have relished every run, every morning, I was almost always eager to listen to something new by Zacharias, Begg, or Keller. I had explored a fair bit about God, but much of what I started to question in the Apostles' Creed was about Jesus. Even if I was becoming persuaded about the existence of God based upon the cosmological, design, and moral arguments, how was I to make the link to Christ? I had no doubt that my favorite Christian philosophers would have much to say on that topic as well. So, I continued on.

CHAPTER 8

THE RACE: A NEW START

The hardest thing in the world is to believe in something.
If you do it's a miracle—everyone's trying to talk you out of what
you believe. [Friend: "Do you believe in God?"] I believe in myself.

—Steve Prefontaine (from *Without Limits*)

I was finding the discourse between philosophical positions fascinating; I enjoyed the intellectual pursuit. In some ways, I may have become distracted by a more academic exercise as opposed to a very personal journey. I embraced the moral argument and noted that it pointed to God. But did it point toward the God of the Bible? Did it say anything about Jesus? I was in the midst of this search, seeking answers to many of life's big questions when our daughter Brooke and I went on a medical mission trip to Guatemala.

This was a first for both of us. Randy, my former college roommate and marathon partner back in 1978 and now a cardiologist, led the trip. Randy's daughter and Brooke were now roommates at William & Mary. Curious about medicine as a possible career and, I think, captivated by doing the right thing, Brooke was the catalyst for us to participate in such a trip.

Observing the enormous challenges faced by most Guatemalans and particularly the residents of the remote villages where we ran our medical clinic, I wondered why I had been so fortunate to be

born in the United States. More than that, I was meaningfully
affected by my fellow mission workers, mostly parishioners from
Randy's home church in Lewisburg, Pennsylvania. And our in-
country hosts, the Valdez family, were thoroughly committed
to helping those much less fortunate. In addition to facilitating
our trip and similar mission trips for other groups, the Valdez
family ran what Americans know as a Ronald McDonald house,
only without the corporate funding.

The ministry started decades ago when the Valdezes, at their
own expense, brought coffee and bread to parents and families
sleeping in the streets for weeks or even months while a child or
other family member received medical care. This was some of
the only health care available for the poor in the entire country,
and many walk three, four, or more days just to reach the public
hospital in Guatemala City. Over time, the Valdez family saved
enough to lease a home a couple of blocks away so these families
could have a roof over their head, a bed to sleep in, and three meals
to eat a day. The family matriarch told me that often they have
no idea where the money or food will come from, but they have a
deep faith that God will provide. Some of the stories of need and
deliverance brought tears to my eyes, and also made me face some
of my circumstances of remarkable luck or coincidence—or, as
she assured me, the hand of God.

Before leaving Guatemala, we attended a worship service in
Guatemala City at the home congregation of one of our hosts.
The service, of course, was completely in Spanish. Nonetheless,
I found myself becoming fully engaged and joining in their
exuberance during the worship service. Although I could not
understand but a few words, the songs of praise had a visceral
impact upon me. I teared up. Were these tears of joy (which
happen to me whenever I see a returning soldier surprise his six-
year-old child at school) in response to witnessing the enormous
warmth and happiness being expressed in the music and by the
congregation, or, I wondered, is this something deeper, something
more profound, something that didn't require argument and
reason, something that didn't even require words?

Without planning or searching, I had witnessed a powerful argument for the existence of God in the unselfish devotion to the less fortunate, expressly in the name of Jesus Christ. These new friends were modern-day Good Samaritans. Hence, despite some of my own continuing doubts, the moral argument continued to resonate and keep me engaged in the journey.

One way to describe the process is that the classic arguments seemed to appeal to my head but not my heart. I wanted to know more. My new friends, both native to Guatemala and on the mission team, had clearly found something, and I was pretty sure it wasn't the ontological argument. Why, though, was I having such a struggle resolving these ultimate questions?

A month or so after I returned from Guatemala, while killing time during a two-hour layover in an airport book store, I picked up the book *Misquoting Jesus*,[23] which analyzed the oldest of the existing manuscripts of the New Testament as a way to assess the accuracy of its language as it has been repeated and recopied over the ages. The author, Bart Ehrman, asked, "What is it that we really know about the accuracy of the Scriptures?" In short, he attempted to address what conclusions could reasonably be drawn from looking at verifiable facts about the oldest available versions of the New Testament.

The book suggested a process that I thought might prove fruitful in my own thinking. Like Ehrman, I began to ask the most basic question, "What is it that I know, *really know*, about God or Christ?" I thought this might establish some basics upon which I could build a foundation and curb my doubts. In a way, this was my own form of Descartes' famous analysis of the problem of knowledge where he asked how we could reasonably conclude that we know anything. I recalled learning in freshman Philosophy 101 that Descartes reduced everything, at least initially, to the only thing he thought he could not doubt: "I think, therefore, I am." From there Descartes tried to build a framework or foundation on what he *knew*.

I thought if it was good enough for Descartes, it was certainly good enough for me. So I wondered what about God and Jesus Christ I could comfortably and confidently say I really *knew*. As I considered this question, I ran across websites and blogs contending that Jesus is merely a myth, a variation on or amalgamation of ancient pagan stories or, even a hoax. Obviously, then, the most basic of all questions was whether Jesus actually had ever existed.

While that question might seem odd or even absurd to some, I surmised that the omnipresence of Christian symbols and traditions in American society might allow us to assume or presuppose Jesus existed without really addressing the issue. We say things like "God willing," "I will keep you in my prayers," or "There but for the grace of God, go I." We celebrate Christmas and Easter, count our years from the birth of Christ, and designate dates Before Christ (BC) and *Anno Domini* (AD, for the Latin, "In the year of our Lord," that is, after Christ). These can seduce us into assuming that Jesus existed without stopping long enough to assess the facts that underlie that assumption.

To put it another way, in his essay "Why I am not a Christian," British atheist Bertrand Russell said this: "Historically, it is quite doubtful whether Christ ever existed at all, and if He did we do not know anything about Him."[24]

Was Russell correct?

On the one hand almost 2,000 years after his death, millions of individuals all over the world not only believe He lived, but also recognize Him as Lord, God, and Savior. On the other hand, history is full of instances of long-held beliefs, such as the belief that the sun revolves around the earth, which were later corrected or rejected. The lawyer in me would not likely be persuaded merely by the fact that many people have believed something for a very long time. This did not seem, in itself, to be a sufficient basis to draw any final conclusion about the truth of that belief. So I pressed on, asking about the grounds for this belief.

I began with the obvious. The Bible purports to be a historical record that, among other things, recounts the birth, life, and death of Jesus. Why doesn't that end the inquiry? If I were asking the same question about Julius Caesar or Alexander the Great, wouldn't I simply consult with the historical texts? Thus, the real question was whether I could trust the accuracy of the Gospels and other books of the New Testament. I jumped, therefore, into studying the reliability of the Bible, a topic with a vast body of work.

After some brief reading, I realized I had to be very careful with what scholars mean by "reliable" or "reliability." First, I had to ask whether the words in the New Testament are reliable; that is, do they accurately transmit what the Gospel writers first wrote without errors that may have crept in by human error or intention? Second, even if the words are reliable, could they be accepted as an accurate record of what really happened? Skeptics point out that the Gospel writers, after all, had an agenda and may have written the story in the way best to promote the new Christian faith rather than to communicate the actual facts. Thus, I also wanted to know about the possible existence of third-party sources that corroborated the facts reported in the Gospels.

The basic question presented by *Misquoting Jesus* is whether we are reading accurate copies (or copies of copies of copies) of what these early historians wrote because we don't have any of the original manuscripts. Ehrman emphasizes scribal errors and inconsistencies in the manuscripts that survive. He is skeptical, and these "variants" are what not only caused him to question the accuracy of the biblical story but also to question his own Christian faith.

In addition to Ehrman, I read both popular and more scholarly works on the topic of whether we can trust the Gospels. Of the many questions and concerns I raised on my faith journey, this turned out to be one of the easier ones to resolve.

Oversimplifying their work, I discovered that Bible scholars point to the remarkably insignificant alterations or differences in light of the enormous number of manuscripts. Not to overemphasize this point, but it was enlightening especially for someone like me who considered himself an amateur historian to realize how little we question the accuracy of other ancient history even though our sources are considerably less reliable than those of the Bible. For instance, no one appears to question historical accounts of Caesar, even though the most recent text of *Gallic Wars,* the primary original source for information about his life and activities, was produced more than 1,000 years after he died. Moreover, only ten copies of that work exist. By contrast, we have over 24,000 manuscripts of the New Testament; the earliest one produced about twenty-five years after Jesus' death.

Despite the claims or popularity of *Misquoting Jesus,* very little serious scholarship questions the basic reliability of the Bible. Bible scholar Gleason Archer argued that even after examining all the scribal errors and variants, "No decently attested variant would make the slightest difference in the doctrinal teaching of Scripture if it were substituted for the wording of the approved text."[25] It would be like a judge saying to me after arguing a point, "So what difference does it make for this case, even if you are correct?"

Despite the apparent problems highlighted by *Misquoting Jesus,* after examining the evidence I came to the same conclusion of the vast majority of biblical scholars. I decided that, in terms of the fidelity of the transmission over the years, the New Testament is not only reliable, but also far more reliable than any other ancient text.

If I could confidently conclude that the words written in the Bible are essentially original and that they have not been altered, logically the question became whether they record historical events—people, places, and things—the way they actually existed and occurred. If they do, I could conclude that the Jesus of the Bible is the "historical Jesus." In addition to the four Gospels, the New Testament contains the letters written by Jesus' early followers. Since it would be irrational to argue that we do not have a historical record of Jesus, the real question, like a jury considering a case put to it, is whether we have a reasonable doubt about the accuracy of what is written.

Initially, the scholars who have made these questions their life's work reminded me that while the Gospels are not contemporaneous reports created during Jesus' life, they were written by eyewitnesses or by individuals who had access to eyewitnesses. Moreover, they were prepared in the fifty to one hundred years immediately following Christ's death, a period of time scholars indicate enhances reliability and is inconsistent with the creation of myths or folklore. And the Gospel writers *intended* that their writings be a historical record. Note particularly, the introductory paragraphs of Luke's Gospel:

> *. . . since I myself have carefully investigated everything from the beginning, it seemed good also to me to write an orderly account for you, most excellent Theophilus, so that you may know the certainty of the things you have been taught (Luke 1:3–4).*

We can fairly say that Luke took his job seriously and endeavored to get it right. As one of Paul's traveling companions, Luke had access to the eyewitness testimony of many of the apostles and others who had first-hand accounts.

Bart Ehrman and others suggest that the reader must discount what Luke, Paul, and other believers recorded because they had a very specific agenda. They had a story they wanted to tell for a very specific purpose; thus this bias makes their writings less authentic or credible, so we should doubt their accuracy. Others suggest that the Gospels were written many years after Christ's death to fit the objectives of the early Church rather than to record what actually happened.

Among the rejoinders is that the better evidence demonstrates the Gospels were written within a fairly short period after Christ's death. Moreover, history doesn't provide any reports that give us a different version of the facts from the official biblical accounts. In fact, ancient texts written by secular historians confirm that Jesus lived as a real person in history. Among these sources are Tacitus's *Annals* and Josephus's *Antiquities of the Jews*, which independently record events of Jesus' life; they confirm, therefore, that Jesus really lived and died. Tacitus was a non-Christian historian and Roman senator who lived between A.D. 55 and 120, and Josephus was a Jewish historian who lived at about the same times as Tacitus. My research identified many other secular references to Jesus' life and crucifixion.

That said, the charge that the Gospel writers probably had some level of bias because they had become followers of Christ seemed to make some sense. I thought I should explore this potential problem.

One podcast challenged me by asking whether the Gospel writers were always biased toward Jesus. When they first encountered Jesus were they biased? What Jesus said and did was not what they expected. Thus, they would have been inclined to doubt; that is Jesus' contemporaries would be biased *against* him. The fact that they became so convinced that Jesus was Lord that they were compelled to record the facts of his life doesn't seem to be or even suggest any form of improper bias. Rather, it appears to emphasize the conviction of the beliefs they developed.

My own experience suggested that, for followers of Christ, the sacredness of the task of recording his life would make their reports even more credible, more reliable, not less. I recalled a time I was asked to serve as one of my church's first lay assistants for Communion. I was pretty sure I was selected for political reasons—to help overcome some final passive resistance within the congregation. Nonetheless I agreed. I did not consider it a big deal spiritually, theologically, or politically. Yet, when I donned the robe and participated in the Communion service, I was surprised at how humbling it was to be in and around the altar and to be part of the sacrament. Regardless of how I felt about my faith, Communion was a sacred event and my participation in it was sobering.

Thinking back on that experience, I reasoned that a first century witness to Christ, especially one who undertook the task of reporting the events and words of his life, would be considerably *more* motivated to respect the details and accuracy due to the enormously serious and sacred nature of the task. Moreover, criticism focused on bias or agenda might make sense in a more commercial context, where material gain and prestige may be implicated, but the Gospel writers not only received no pecuniary advantage from recording the life of Jesus. Instead, they were persecuted and faced execution for their allegiance to someone viewed by Roman and Jewish society as a rabble-rouser and a heretic.

I became convinced, therefore, that the writers' faith had caused them not to invent or embellish but (just as Luke said) to be *very* careful to get it right—to set things down objectively and accurately out of respect and humility, if not fear. Having experienced Christ first-hand or through eye-witness accounts and being convinced about the truth of Jesus Christ, a more likely conclusion is that Luke and the other Gospel writers would, in fact, be even *more* motivated to take assiduous care to make sure they recorded everything correctly. This story was not some happy fantasy or historical novel; it was, after all, the life and times and death and resurrection of the writers' Lord and Savior.

Further, an omniscient God, whom you anticipate seeing at Judgment Day, will know what is true and what is not true. Addressing and commenting on something as important—as sacred—as the story of Christ would sober any believer to want to be true to the actual story, true to the truth. For a Gospel writer to alter or embellish the story to fit *his* idea of the story of Jesus (that he knew better how to shape that story) would suggest a level of arrogance inconsistent with his faith. Moreover, as people were transformed by their belief in Christ, those writers would see the task at hand to be a sacred mission; they would never think to trifle with the details or the truth.

In addition to evaluating the motivation of the New Testament writers in recording the events they purported to see, I learned that formal, textual analysis of ancient writings also supports the accuracy and credibility of those events. In attempting to explain the problems with the copies or "variants" of the Bible,

Bart Ehrman provides the reader with a primer on textual criticism in the earlier chapters of *Misquoting Jesus*, including an explanation of the tests of dissimilarity, independent attestation, and contextual credibility. More specifically, Ehrman explains that the criterion or test of "dissimilarity" (often referred to as the "criterion of embarrassment") helps to demonstrate that certain facts or details are more likely to be true or accurate. For instance, if a fact or tradition in question in a text works against or is adverse to the interests of those that preserved it, this "test" provides that such fact or tradition is more likely to be historically reliable—it is more likely to have happened. Thus, because various events preserved in the Gospels that are "embarrassing"—that do not reflect well on early Christians—the "test" suggests that such facts are more likely to be true.

One commonly noted example is the presence and role of women in Jesus' life. Women are frequent witnesses to various events, including some of the most crucial. Mary, the mother of James, Mary Magdalene, and Joanna were at the tomb on Easter morning—the first to be witness to the bodily resurrection. But in the first century women could not give testimony in courts of law. Due to women's lowly status, no one would put women in the numerous significant events and make them important witnesses unless what they were writing was in fact true.

Similarly, incidents are reported that do not reflect favorably on Jesus or the disciples. Peter and James selfishly lobbied to be the most favored disciples. The disciples fell asleep while Jesus struggled in prayer with his waning hours. Peter denied Jesus a few hours later. The early leaders of the Church look pretty pathetic in some of the pages of the Gospels.

Another observation made by some scholars that I found compelling was that Jesus' death was by crucifixion. Death by crucifixion would do little to engender confidence in this new religion; the first-century Jews and Gentiles knew crucifixion was a punishment reserved for the lowliest of criminals, certainly not a holy figure they should worship. (Crucifixion was so horrible no one who was a Roman citizen could be subjected to it.) Thus, as the argument goes, if you were going to fabricate or embellish the story of Jesus, you certainly would not write it as it was written. The events recorded in the Gospels are more likely to be historically reliable because they work against the objectives of the early Christian movement and are otherwise embarrassing or awkward for the early church.

If I were honest with myself, therefore, I would not find difficulty in accepting the accuracy of the factual and historical material found in the Gospels. Even easier was to be confident that we have a solid basis to conclude that Jesus, at a minimum, was a real person of history.

Despite Bertrand Russell's assertion, when all was said and done, to determine that Jesus was an actual, historical figure was not difficult. That Jesus lived and traveled around Palestine as, at least, an itinerant speaker is not a seriously disputed matter. In fact, even the religions of Judaism and Islam, which reject Christ as the Messiah or as God, acknowledge that he *did* exist. Similarly, historically prominent atheists like H.G. Wells and the modern biologist Richard Dawkins, acknowledge that the evidence that Christ was a historical person is persuasive. More to the point, biblical scholar Otto Betz states unequivocally "No serious scholar has ventured to postulate the non-historicity of Jesus."[26] Finally, F.F. Bruce, one of the world's foremost Bible scholars, and one who mentored Bart Ehrman, has written:

> *Some writers may toy with the 'Christ-myth,' but they do not do so on the ground of historical evidence. The historicity of Christ is as axiomatic for the unbiased historian as the historicity of Julius Caesar.*[27]

Stated simply, therefore, I was able to conclude that I had something to stand on—at least "one thing" I *knew* about Jesus. I now recognized that I had very good reasons to trust the accuracy of the events recorded in the Gospels. In fact, with a high degree of confidence, I concluded that, as a matter of historical fact, a man we refer to as Jesus Christ lived over 2,000 years ago. With that solid, first building block, the next step seemed rather obvious. Yes, I could conclude that Jesus had existed, but was he who he said he was—was he divine, God's chosen son, the "Son of Man?"

Once I concluded that the story of Christ is neither a good piece of fiction nor interesting folklore and that Christ was a real person who lived, the next step logically would be to assess the extent to which the things recorded about his life—his teachings, miracles, and life events—are also true. Thus, I quickly realized that I was reaching a point where I could now only conclude one of two things. I had a simple, but frightening choice: either Jesus *was* the Son of God, or he was a lunatic. This is not meant to be flippant or disrespectful. The phrasing of this sharp contrast is not mine, but it is purposeful here. And I think this was part of what was nagging me when I read the Apostles' Creed or the Nicene Creed each week; if I believed the words, shouldn't my reaction to them be different? And in some respects, if I did *not* believe them, what was I doing standing there each Sunday reciting something I knew I did not believe?

The choice between God and lunatic, of course, is not original. That is the way I heard other commentators set out the options. Tim Keller explained in one of his sermons that if you are going to walk around and tell people you are the son of God and that no one comes to God except through you, either you are crazy or you are the son of God—can you think of any other explanation? I later realized that this phrasing came from C.S. Lewis who said that same thing, in this particularly powerful manner:

> *Either this man was, and is, the Son of God: or else a madman or something worse. You can shut Him up for a fool, you can spit at Him and kill Him as a demon; or you can fall at His feet and call Him Lord and God. But let us not come with any patronizing nonsense about Him being a great human teacher. He has not left that open to us. He did not intend to.*[28]

So that's the ultimate question. Having concluded that one thing I knew was that Jesus was a real person of history, these questions obviously followed: If Jesus Christ actually existed, was he also the Son of Man? Was he God? He had existed, but did He exist today? How can I find the answer these questions? How can I determine if Jesus is Lord or lunatic? I wondered, what would persuade me that Jesus was who he claimed to be?

One morning, with a Tim Keller sermon between my ears, I settled on a very simple approach to this question involving the resurrection. If that event really occurred, wouldn't it be some of the best evidence, if not the very best evidence, that Christ is who he said he was and who the Church believes him to be? If God intervened in history to raise Christ from the dead just as he predicted (and appeared to the Apostles, Paul, and others) would not such a supernatural event be a sufficient explanation, a sufficient validation, that Jesus is Lord? It would, in fact, be compelling if not completely conclusive. I thought I had a good approach, but how could I get at this simple, but profound question?

CHAPTER 9

HALFWAY (13.1 MILES)

... under the sun the race is not to the swift, nor the battle to the strong, nor bread to the wise, nor riches to the intelligent, nor favor to those with knowledge, but time and chance happen to them all.

—Ecclesiastes 9:11

Just as my study of apologetics led me from argument to argument, my efforts to develop as a runner took a similar path. I started signing up for and running in other local races. I was not eager to compete. Running for me was personal, and I was not out to see how many people finished behind me. I ran in the Race for the Cure 5K and the Carytown 10K the next month and set my sights on a half-marathon. I used these local races as a tactic to combat my lack of discipline, if not my natural laziness. Not only did it make a good workout, but also if I was going to commit to another 10K or half-marathon (or a marathon), I had to keep up my training in order to have a good race. Forcing myself to get out and train would obviously help me along the way. And, perhaps most important for me, if I signed up for a race and told people that I had, I'd be embarrassed if I then slacked off (as I was clearly prone to do) or didn't post for the run.

The Marathon Training Team schedule expects a member to run a half-marathon at the end of the summer. Richmond has its Patrick Henry Half in Ashland, and the Rock 'n Roll half-marathon on Labor Day weekend is in Virginia Beach, about two hours away. After the Monument Avenue 10K, I had accepted the invitation from a few of my law partners who are real runners to run the Virginia Beach race with them.

Shortly before that race, I played golf with a couple of friends; our fourth, Jeff, was a new acquaintance. The topic of running came up. My naïveté about running also came up, again. Jeff had run the Richmond marathon recently. I explained to him that I was a very new runner, was getting ready for my first 13.1-mile race, and was going to try to run the New York marathon in a few months. Jeff offered me encouragement and asked if I was using a Garmin. I asked what that was, and he explained that it was a watch to wear while running. Linked to a satellite, the GPS watch would measure pace and distance as well as time. He suggested a good website for running gear. I gave it some thought for a few days, and then took the plunge and purchased a Garmin Forerunner 305. I used that watch for almost every subsequent training run or race.

I had done a pretty good job through the summer keeping up my miles, including an increasingly long run each Wednesday that would get up to ten miles before tapering off in preparation for the full marathon in November. So by Labor Day, I had booked some good miles and had several runs of eight to ten miles in the bank. While I felt generally prepared for 13.1 miles, that was still a long distance to run.

My law partner, Mike, and I made the two-hour drive to Virginia Beach to meet up with a couple of partners from our offices in Tidewater. After connecting with Steve, who would host us for the weekend, we picked up Ray and headed over to get our bibs and timing chips for the next day's race. The Virginia Beach Rock 'n Roll Half-Marathon is run by Elite Racing, which conducts numerous race events throughout the U.S. This company brings a high level of organization and professionalism to what has become a major half-marathon.

This was my first real runners' "expo" where race participants pick up their bibs, chips, race shirts, and a variety of giveaways, discount coupons, and flyers, all delivered in a bag that is then used to drop off excess clothing and other items prior to the race. Once the bag is dropped off, someone like Federal Express or UPS magically whisks the bags to a staging area near the finish line. A big runners' expo also features booths promoting races throughout the county and the world, running products from shoes to shirts to specially formulated drinks, as well as retail outlets for running gear and race memorabilia. Many of the larger expos feature a running personality or two such as multiple Boston Marathon winner Bill Rogers, ultra-marathoner Dean Karnazes, or Olympic Marathon Gold medal winner Frank Shorter.

At Virginia Beach, Shorter hosted some Q & A sessions for runners to ask about training, nutrition, equipment, and other running-related question. Toward the end of our tour around the booths selling gels and Gu, I was speaking with someone at a booth about the Nashville Country Music Marathon when Mike came up, tapped me on the shoulder and said, "Come on, we have to go. We're taking Frank Shorter back to his hotel."

"Frank Shorter?" I exclaimed, "*The* Frank Shorter?"

Yes, *the* Frank Shorter. As we drove him to his hotel, we asked him about Ryan Hall—the great, new American hope in the marathon—and other topics. We dropped him off at The Cavalier Hotel, and as we pulled away, I said to my three partners in the car, "We should have invited him to dinner."

General agreement followed and almost as quickly Steve said, "No problem, I'll call him, I got his number."

To make a long story a little shorter (pun intended), we took Frank to dinner and listened to fascinating stories of running in the 1970s, training with Steve Prefontaine, the Munich Olympics including the Israel hostage crisis, his silver medal in the 1976 Olympics for which he still expects to receive the Gold as the truth about East Germany drug doping is brought to light, and the International Anti-Doping Commission of which Shorter was a founding member. It was an amazing and entertaining evening.

After dinner, bed. I certainly thought I would need a good night's rest to face 13.1 miles in the morning.

I woke after a pretty good sleep, dressed carefully, and came downstairs in my law partner's home for breakfast. Steve's wife had an assortment of breakfast foods for us, but I had brought my own bagel, banana, and peanut butter. These preparations about my pre-race meal generated plenty of comments about becoming a real runner-geek. I shrugged them off. I had a long run to worry about, and at that point the worry was getting to me.

After fueling up, we gathered with another partner and some other friends, crammed into a minivan, and headed toward the start at the conference center, just a few blocks short of the oceanfront. After a fifteen-minute drive, we hopped out onto the expressway and traveled the last quarter mile by foot joining more than 14,000 others for this Rock 'n Roll weekend.

My running buddy Dan had also come down for the Virginia Beach half. We ran it together finishing in two hours thirteen minutes, which was just about a 10-minute pace. I was very pleased. After the race, Dan went off to find his much faster wife, and I headed off to find my much faster partners. Later, I learned that after we parted, Dan had all but collapsed from dehydration. Thankfully, he recovered well and we continued to train together.

I had completed my first half-marathon; and although my pace was slow, I had come a long way in eight months with a marathon nine weeks away. Something that seemed highly improbable was starting to seem possible. Or did it really? I had run 13.1 miles, but when I finished—though pleased—I thought I could never run that distance again plus another 13.1 miles. Finishing the Rock 'n Roll Half seemed to have taken everything I had. At the same time, I had come a long way. I still had lots of miles to log as the MTT began to run fourteen, fifteen, eighteen, and twenty miles, but I trusted the MTT system. Maybe I could run the marathon.

So I kept up with the MTT schedule. About a month after the Virginia Beach race, I discovered another opportunity to run a half-marathon.

The McDonald's Half is part of a weekend-long cross-country festival at Richmond's Maymont Park. So I signed up. Why not get another race experience under my belt? This became one of my mental training aids; I would sign up for races so I always had another race coming up. With less than excellent self-control and discipline, signing up for races helped keep me honest. If I always have another distance race upcoming and I tell people, I have to keep training so I will be prepared and won't have to tell my friends I had quit.

The McDonald's Half turned out to be a great run. I felt comfortable and strong throughout the race, which featured some of downtown Richmond's more beautiful streets, especially the ones along and across the James River. At the end I still had a lot of energy. In fact, with a mile to go I upped my pace to see how well I could finish and, beginning to bleed from one of my nipples, I completed the last mile in eight minutes while the overall pace was a little better than typical at almost exactly ten minutes per mile. "Wow! That was a good run," I said to myself, surprised at how good I felt after running more than 13 miles.

As difficult as I found completing twelve or fourteen miles to be, I was now running farther than I had dreamed possible at the start of the year. Maybe I could finish a marathon! Confidence was beginning to build. One thing that helped prepare me for these longer runs was the MTT schedule, which I followed fairly religiously. Staying on course required some determination, but I probably could not have done it on my own. Having a running buddy or being part of a weekly group are a big help for those of us inclined to backslide and try to take a day or two off. As we got closer to the day of the marathon, the weekly mid-week run grew in length. Completing those runs, which got up to nine and ten miles near the end, helped provide a crucial base. Thankfully, Dan had encouraged me to join him in that early morning group without which I wondered if I would have had the resolve to run that far mid-week.

⚶ ⚶ ⚶ ⚶ ⚶

"Car up!" If you are outside the streets in Richmond's Fan District on Saturday mornings, you are likely to hear this yelp. It's a runner's way to warn other runners that a car is coming. Not surprisingly, hearing such warnings can be difficult if one is listening to an MP3 player and wearing earphones. And, while the opportunity to listen to music, a sermon, or an audio book is important, safety on the streets is important as well. As a new runner, I learned quickly, like a parent weighing the choice between public and private schooling for their children, that people had many opinions, freely offered, about running with an iPod.

One friend who knew I had started running told me, "Running is too boring. I could never do it without listening to music on my iPod." Others explained how they enjoyed getting away in their own world by listening to tunes. In contrast, many runners eschew any use of listening devices. Purists of the anti-iPod contingent think that music in your ears disturbs the tranquility of a good run.

I agreed strongly with both camps. I understood the solitude of a run, enjoying the outdoors and the time to work things through my mind uninterrupted by outside noise. On the other hand, I also enjoyed listening to music, especially with a busy schedule that leaves little time for such pleasures. In addition, I had my podcasts and enjoyed the efficiency of getting a chance to listen to a great moment in history or a new sermon while also getting some exercise in. So, as I said, I felt strongly both ways.

A couple of weeks after the McDonald's Half, the MTT Saturday run was up to eighteen miles. I had a conflict and couldn't run with the group. Fortunately, the next day the Scholarship 30K—18.3 miles—was being held at Pocahontas Park south of Richmond. Participating in the race was a perfect opportunity for me to stay on schedule. The local running club sponsors the race at that time of year to attract the many runners training for the Richmond marathon or other fall marathons such as The Marine Corps in D.C., the New York, and the Chicago.

The Scholarship race offers 10K, 20K and a 30K option, meaning that it's one, two, or three loops around a 6.2-mile course on dirt paths in Pocahontas State Park. This race was not only the longest distance I would attempt in decades, but it was off-road, somewhat hilly, and a little redundant. A single loop whether it was three miles or thirteen was more attractive than doing many loops around a track or anything else.

Because my running buddy Dan would not be with me, I decided to experiment with listening to music during a race to practice, to fight some of the potential monotony, and to help the time go by. I found my way to the race site and walked near the start line with my earphones and iPod ready to go.

Experienced runners, running coaches, and many running books will say that you shouldn't experiment with anything on race day! Anything new should be tried out well before a race. You need to know that your shorts won't chafe in the wrong place, your shirt is comfortable, and your shoes are tried and true. You also shouldn't experiment with a new meal the morning of a race. Taking this advice to heart, as mentioned, I had brought my own banana and peanut butter to my host's home for the Virginia Beach half-marathon. My law partners had a good laugh on my account, including the pronouncement from Mike, "You're a real runner geek now."

Anticipating that I might want to use my iPod during my first marathon, however, I thought this would be a good opportunity to try it. That was until I met the iPod Nazi. At the starting area, about four hundred runners gathered. I had my iPod and earphones. Then I heard a raspy, obnoxious, and exceedingly loud voice that reminded me of a *Seinfeld* character demanding that everyone remove their earphones, insisting that it was a matter of safety to run without distraction from such instruments of death as iPods.

In 2008 the United States Track & Field Association took a stand on this issue by amending Rule 144.3 to provide that the race director for a particular event, at his sole discretion, may permit such devices (provided they cannot receive communications) excepting those individuals competing for prizes in the race. Previously the USTF had prohibited the devices without qualification.

I was disappointed and unconvinced that this was some safety issue. After all, this race was three laps of the same 10K course, and the entire course was within a state park, on dirt trails where no vehicles were permitted.

So, at a minute before the start, I had to tear off my earphones and find a place to stash my iPod since I didn't have time to get to my car and back for the start. Needless to say, that was not the type of last minute change that helps mental race preparation.

Nonetheless, I ran the first two loops fairly well for me. Then halfway through the last loop, at about mile fifteen, I started to fade. My legs got heavy. Rather than thinking about work or family or vacations or golf trips, all I could think about (other than inappropriate thoughts about the iPod Nazi) was how tired I was becoming. I believed that "real runners" do not walk. Yet, there I was—spent. I gave in and decided to walk for a few minutes. I hated to do it. It made me feel inadequate and caused me to question the progress I thought I had made.

After some walking and some running, I walked up the steep hill near the finish and then, out of pride if nothing else, I mustered enough strength to run the last quarter mile crossing the finish in three hours forty minutes—a pace of twelve minutes. I was a little disappointed, but that was the furthest I had run in thirty years. It was good and bad. I finished without too much trouble, but I was clearly starting to crash. How would I ever do that and then another eight miles?

As a business bankruptcy lawyer, because of its money center banks and preferred venue for Chapter 11 filings, I inevitably travel to New York City at times for business. A month or so before the New York City Marathon, I had a meeting with bankers in Manhattan. As we started our landing sequence into LaGuardia, the plane was diverted east and then had to circle back for a second attempt. This diversion brought us right over Manhattan on a beautiful day. With the marathon much on my mind, I knew that the finish was right there, five thousand feet below me in Central Park. I was excited as I looked down at the park and dreamed about finishing the twenty-six miles there.

The next morning I dressed for a run and excitedly began to jog toward the Plaza Hotel, where I knew of an easy entrance into Central Park. I was amazed at the number of walkers, runners, dog walkers, and bikers in the park at 6:15. Central Park has a main loop road that covers most of the park. My run took me from the southeast corner up to the northeast corner, over to the northwest corner, and back south. Apparently New York has no rule, written or unwritten, as to whether the walking, running, and cycling traffic should go clockwise or counterclockwise. I headed out counterclockwise along the east side near 5th Avenue and then heading north toward Harlem. My fellow runners were of every shape and size. Young, twenty-something professionals keeping a pace I wish I could run for one mile, let alone five or ten (or twenty-six); older men, some running at remarkably brisk paces and others at near walking paces; and everything in between. I encountered groups of two or three, lots of women, people coming toward me, others passing me. And, every few moments, a group of two or four or ten bike riders would fly by.

Almost immediately after I got on the loop road, I began to pass runners coming toward me. Being a polite southerner (despite my distinct Yankee roots), I waved good morning. No response. So I waved at the next few runners I passed. Again, no responses. This jarred my mood a bit. Here I was running in New York on a beautiful fall morning, thinking about returning in a month for the marathon. I was taking in the Metropolitan Museum of Art, glancing at the CNN Tower and a mosaic of other tall buildings bordering the park, and trying to fit it all into the fabric of a morning in perhaps the greatest urban park in the world, and I got no response.

During my next Saturday run with Dan, I mentioned the lack of any reply to my waves to the runners in Central Park. I hypothesized that, just as collegiality among local lawyers decreases as the size of the local bar increases, friendliness and civility decreases as the community of runners increases. I was amazed by the consistent failure or refusal to return a simple wave. So we did our own survey as we ran through the streets of Richmond.

That morning we did a fairly long run that took us over the Huguenot Bridge and down the south side of the James River. That is a popular running route, perhaps the prettiest run in Richmond, so we were far from alone. Although we typically waved to most people we saw, that day we made a special effort to wave to oncoming runners and to keep track of who and how many responded. We found that an overwhelming majority— approximately eighty percent—responded positively with a return wave. Maybe Richmond is, as the slogan for the Richmond Marathon suggests, the friendliest running town.

This story reminds me of another observation Dan and I routinely shared with each other as we continued on our journey toward the marathon with the MTT. As a new and intimidated runner, I was incredibly impressed with the MTT program, the coaches, and my fellow runners because of the support I received. Very few focused on his or her time or on being first. Everyone we knew was welcoming and supportive. I started thinking and then commenting to Dan, "Runners are good people."

A year later, as I shared a few miles with Faith, my MTT coach and an employee of Richmond Sports Backers, I learned that Richmond might be the town with the greatest race participation. Apparently, Chicago has the greatest overall number of participants, but on a per capita basis, Richmond far exceeded any other U.S. city with almost a thousand individuals registered and running with the MTT.

The Chicago marathon training team program was featured in a Nova special on PBS called *Marathon Challenge* (available on Netflix). That program is almost identical to the Richmond Sports Backers program of which I was part. Almost at the very same time that the *Marathon Challenge* became available on DVD, another inspirational running movie called *The Spirit of the Marathon* debuted at major motion picture theaters. It only ran a few days, but Mike and I made plans and attended together.

At the theater, we ran into Kathy, a fellow runner who always had a supportive word for me, who again encouraged me in my pursuit. Kathy had been profiled a couple of years earlier in our local paper as they followed her in her effort to run the Richmond Marathon as she battled back from cancer. When she wasn't running in an event, she was a volunteer wherever she might be needed. I still recall her encouragement, a year or so later, as she handed me some water around mile nine of a very hot, half-marathon at a time I was struggling terribly. She exemplified what I was observing in my new running community—a selfless passion to help others and support their efforts to achieve a goal. To me, Kathy was a runner. (Sadly, Kathy's cancer returned and she died a year later.)

With the MTT, we had worked through a sixteen-mile and an eighteen-mile run. Now it was time to attempt the longest training run of the program before we started a taper for the last two weeks before race day. I never would have believed that I could do fifteen or sixteen miles—never mind twenty miles, but here we were getting ready to go that distance.

The weather that Saturday morning was fair, neither hot nor cool. We worked through the miles as we had for our earlier runs, although the last two or three were tough—Dan started to experience some lower leg cramping, and I was exhausted. Our pace fell off. Nonetheless, we finished without needing to walk any of the distance. We then enjoyed one of my favorite parts of these runs: we traded sweat soaked dry-fit shirts for clean, cotton T-shirts. We drank some water and Gatorade, congratulated each other, wished each other well for the upcoming week, and hopped in our cars.

I had driven west toward home about a mile when I saw an MTT friend—a fifty-year-old mother, who was still finishing her twenty miles. I had finished almost an hour before she did, but I looked out and smiled with pure joy knowing that she had persevered and was going to complete the distance as well. She kept her pace and finished the task. I may have been as happy for her as she was. Maybe I was becoming a runner too.

CHAPTER 10

COLSON'S PROOF: RUNNING FROM WATERGATE

I believe that God made me for a purpose—for China [mission work],
but he also made me fast! And when I run I feel his pleasure....
To give it up would be to hold Him in contempt....
It's not just fun—to win, is to honor Him.

—Eric Liddell (from *Chariots of Fire*)

The distance I had traveled on both my physical journey and my spiritual journey was considerable. Not only had my conditioning reached a point where completing the marathon was a possibility and perhaps now even within sight, but I also learned that I had a spot in the ING New York City Marathon. Just as I was enthused about the race potential, I was excited about how far I had come in examining my faith. I sensed that I was close to the finish. In fact, I now had what I thought would be the final, ultimate question.

Little could be more compelling, I thought, than to become convinced of the truth of Christ's resurrection. It is so central to the Christian faith that the apostle Paul wrote, "If Christ was not raised from the dead then your faith is in vain" (1 Corinthians 15:17). The objective was very clear: How to become convinced that the resurrection really happened.

If we are trying to determine whether the Greeks prevailed at the battle of Marathon, we are most apt to check a history book, which supplies the answer. I had become comfortable with the reliability of the Bible. Thus, because the Bible reports the resurrection, was that sufficient evidence? With little thought or analysis though, I had concluded that such an approach, without more evidence, wasn't working for me. But why not?

On deeper reflection, I recognized that my reluctance to accept the resurrection as a historical event just because it is recorded in the Bible was because the "record" was not merely the account of a territorial conquest or genealogical fact. Rather, the event that concerned me was supernatural—a miracle. Was considering whether a man was raised from the dead even rational? It was part of the Apostles' Creed, but was it real—could it be true? Wasn't an actual bodily resurrection just too unbelievable? Wouldn't it violate the laws of nature? I wondered, therefore, how we could determine if the resurrection of Christ was true, if it had actually occurred.

I took a mental step back and asked how we could know any fact in history. How do we know, for example, about Magellan's travels or Caesar's conquests? How do we know that Washington defeated Cornwallis or that the Greeks defeated the Persians at Marathon?

As I thought about these issues, I recalled a curious observation about establishing the truthfulness of the resurrection. At least fifteen years earlier, a friend loaned me a set of cassette tapes by Charles Colson. What I remember most from those tapes was one entitled, "Watergate Proves the Resurrection." With such a provocative title, no wonder I remembered it fifteen years later. But I wondered what Watergate could possibly have to do with whether Jesus had been raised from the dead. I looked around for sources that might recall Colson's proof.

Colson had been one of President Nixon's henchmen who allegedly orchestrated bad acts (dirty tricks), including the Watergate burglary, allegedly in an effort to help assure Nixon's re-election in 1972. After being convicted of obstruction of justice, Colson served seven months of a one- to-three-year sentence in prison. Prior to this conviction Colson professed his faith in Christ, and after his release from prison, began a ministry known as Prison Fellowship, which brings the Gospel to people incarcerated throughout the world.

(A point of personal privilege here. Early in my long run of faith, with a derisive, if not self-righteous tone, I asked my friend Carl if Colson's conversion was legitimate or merely convenient— since it came on the eve of his sentencing and incarceration. Having now read a few of Colson's books [including his very personal and powerful conversion story, *Born Again*, and having followed his ministry since then, I owe him an apology, which I make here. Charles Colson has been a tireless, evangelist for over thirty years. His ministry, Prison Fellowship, is a remarkable endeavor. I should hope to aspire to be Chuck Colson. I had no business judging him. Before I was able to share this apology with him, Chuck Colson died in April of 2012].)

Colson contrasted the actions of Nixon's closest lieutenants after their leader had fallen to those of the Apostles after Christ's death. What did Nixon's followers do when called to testify before Congress and at their own trials for criminal conspiracy? They turned against Nixon, pointed fingers at others, and did everything possible to try to protect their own self-interest. In biblical terms, they denied Nixon.

By contrast, what did Christ's followers do after he was crucified? Rather than repudiate Christ to avoid ridicule, persecution and, in many cases, death, they stood by their belief in him as the resurrected Son of God. They started the early church and began to spread the word of Jesus and his teachings. Many of them knowingly and voluntarily went to their deaths— violent, painful, premature deaths—rather than reject Christ or deny that he had been raised. But why? Why didn't the disciples act like Nixon's inner circle? Don't most of us, I observed, react just like Nixon's lieutenants? Doesn't our nature cause us to seek self-preservation at almost any cost? Isn't history filled more with stories of betrayals than martyrdom?

Christian historians and theologians state that Jesus' disciples were surprised by his death—that was not what they were expecting. Rather than anticipating their leader to be brutalized and humiliated and to suffer the most degrading of all deaths, the Apostles expected Jesus to become a great, powerful political leader. If that anticipated state of affairs had been realized, they might well have been the beneficiaries of Jesus' powerful position. They would naturally expect that such status would come with wealth, privilege, and positions of influence (similar to Nixon's lieutenants *before* his disgrace).

In contrast, Jesus was crucified. His followers were persecuted. Being a Christian had no material benefit or political advantage. In fact, respectable society had no place for a Christian. Thus, following an unknown carpenter from Nazareth looked like a very bad decision. Their leader was dead. Both the Jews and the Gentiles rejected them. And as a result of the choice they had made, Christ's followers would be ridiculed and persecuted at best and tortured or killed at worst.

What would you do next? Most probably thought they should start life over. Go back to fishing. Tell the family they were sorry they left to follow some lunatic. Distance themselves from the discredited leader, the group's power structure, and any other followers. And maybe, if they wanted to gain new respect or earn money, they could assist the Jewish and Roman authorities in trying to put an end to these followers of "The Way." But the disciples did not do this. So how *did* they react to Christ's death?

Initially, their response was not very admirable. Peter, like the Watergate witnesses, repudiated Jesus. Others, like the two disciples who encountered Jesus on the road to Emmaus, didn't recognize him. Most refused to believe initially. Thomas asked for more evidence. Yet, shortly after Jesus' death, the disciples recommitted themselves to him. They became leaders of the early church. They became missionaries, established the new churches, and spread the word about Christ. They faced ridicule and rejection rather than achieving power, prestige, or profits.

Our credibility is strained to think that the Apostles adopted, maintained, *and* tried to spread a faith in a disgraced leader where such belief was met by others with derision and where such believers faced being outcast, persecuted, ridiculed and killed, unless they believed in every fiber of their body that the Gospel was true. For these reasons Colson pointed to Watergate as proving the resurrection. He wrote:

> *I know the resurrection is a fact, and Watergate proved it to me. How? Because 12 men testified they had seen Jesus raised from the dead, and then they proclaimed that truth for 40 years, never once denying it. Every one was beaten, tortured, stoned and put in prison. They would not have endured that if it weren't true. Watergate embroiled 12 of the most powerful men in the world—and they couldn't keep a lie for three weeks. You're telling me 12 apostles could keep a lie for 40 years? Absolutely impossible.*[29]

Colson's proof was persuasive, if not compelling. Like a lawyer not wanting to omit any possible argument from an appellate brief, however, I tried to collect all the reasons—all the evidence—that might support the case for the resurrection. The more I inquired and cataloged the reasons, the more I began to conclude, remarkably, that the evidence seemed to be overwhelming that not only did Jesus exist but that he was—incredibly and supernaturally—raised from the dead.

Finally, not only have no known sources been discovered that report facts, observations, or testimonials rejecting the Christian claims, but the strength of those convictions of the first-century Christians appears to have convinced others. Early Christian writers who had no opportunity for eyewitness confirmation— and, therefore, had to accept the extraordinary reports "on faith"— nonetheless helped to preserve and spread the news. For example, about one hundred years after Jesus' death, Justin Martyr was so convinced of the truth of the resurrection—despite not having access to any eyewitnesses—that he wrote some of the earliest Christian apologetics during a time of great persecution and then went to his own death as a martyr for the faith.

I recalled that Charles Colson often said, "People will die for a belief—even if wrongly held—but they will not die for a lie." That resonated with me. If the Apostles *knew* the resurrection was a hoax, such as if they had stolen and hid the body, why would they go to their deaths clinging to unfounded belief? If the Apostles *knew* that they really had not seen and been with Christ after the resurrection—if they had collectively the whole story— would they have wasted their time and endured the ridicule, the persecution, and the suffering? Considering all of the people who would have had to remain silent about the truth—and remain silent while being persecuted, marginalized, tortured, or worse— could they have even kept the story alive?

The early leaders of the Christian church were not alone as the subjects of horrific treatment. At the time of and following Jesus' death, all followers of Christ were ignored, marginalized, persecuted, tortured and killed. To be part of the early Christian church was not popular. The predominant Jewish population and the occupying Romans did not accept or protect early Christian's right to practice the religion of their choosing. A much safer physical and economic route would be to turn their back on this disgraced, defeated, and crucified teacher. In fact, the mistreatment of the members of the early church often became extreme both in terms of the level of persecution and the severity of the physical treatment.

From its inception, Christianity was attacked by the Jewish leaders and rejected by Jewish society. Official, government-sanctioned persecution began at least as early as AD 64 when Emperor Nero blamed the great fire in Rome on the Christians. One of the earliest Christian writers, Polycarp, was arrested for being a Christian—a member of a politically dangerous cult whose rapid growth needed to be stopped. Because he was advanced in age, the Roman authorities apparently took pity on him and agreed to set him free if he would proclaim, "Caesar is Lord." Unwilling to deny Christ (unlike Nixon's inner circle), Polycarp was burned at the stake. Despite such persecution, when the Church was least established, and therefore most vulnerable, thousands—most who had *not* heard or seen Christ personally— became believers and followers.

The continued growth of the early church was also a compelling fact for me. The message of the early believers, and the conviction with which it was shared, must have been amazingly passionate and convincing to help the church survive and grow given the extent to which it was not just unpopular, but considerably dangerous to be known as a follower of Christ.

The official persecution became much more systematic and relentless in A.D. 249 with Emperor Decius, who pursued a campaign to eradicate Christianity completely from the Roman Empire. Yet the Church of Christ grew! Similarly, around A.D. 303–311 Emperor Diocletian led the most organized and brutal state efforts to eliminate the Church. Yet, the Church survived. Formal persecution continued until at least A.D. 313 when Emperor Constantine issued the Edict of Milan that made tolerance the official policy in the Roman world. Finally, in 380 the Edict of Thessalonica made Christianity the official religion of the Roman Empire.

Why did the Apostles and thousands of early Christians live, suffer, and die in this manner? Why did they continue to follow Christ after his death? What happened after Christ's death that might have motivated Paul and the Apostles to proclaim the Word of God and to evangelize in the face of the ridicule, persecution, and death that they almost certainly knew they were going to face if they did not repudiate Christ? And why did followers who never had a first-hand experience with Christ behave in a similar manner?

The only answer that makes any sense, that logic indicates persuasively, and the most rational explanation, is that after Christ was crucified, he was, in fact, raised from the dead and then appeared to the disciples and others, including Paul. The resurrection of Christ was such a momentous event that the disciples had no choice as to what they should do. They told the world, and they told it with such conviction that those who listened but had not seen Christ were also convinced. This explanation becomes compelling. Even the devil's advocate within me had trouble formulating any kind of credible rejoinder.

Recalling the childhood admonition about jumping off bridges, just because someone did or believed something wasn't a convincing reason to do or accept the same thing. I was focused on making a "leap," not because someone else did and not because someone else said so but because I recognized just how well Christian beliefs resonated as true and have stood the test of time. In my profession, after presenting the weight of evidence in support of the resurrection, attorneys arguing the Christian perspective would suggest that any burden of proof had shifted to those who doubt the resurrection to prove otherwise. I couldn't help but wonder and ask just how we reach *any* conclusion in life?

As I considered how compelling this evidence was, I also recalled that in the face of a skeptical culture and competing religions, Christians have affirmed Jesus Christ as Savior and Lord and have maintained that "He was crucified, died and was buried and on the third day raised from the dead." And, more to the point, perhaps no organization, institution, or belief system has been challenged and examined more thoroughly than Christianity—a cross-examination that has lasted for the two millennia since Christ's death. This skepticism aside, skeptics, critics, and atheists don't seem to have developed a credible, alternative explanation to this most central and most crucial of all Christian claims.

The lawyer in me recognized that the evidence behind Colson's proof is not direct but circumstantial. I noted that in my own practice, I had to prove fraudulent transfers almost exclusively through circumstantial evidence. Concerning the resurrection then, the compelling circumstantial evidence is the conduct of the apostles and the other believers after Christ's death. Analyzing all of this intently, I wondered how anyone could suggest a different hypothesis for what happened the first few hundred years after Christ's death or to explain the durability of the Church into the present day?

I read a few books on this topic. A good part of the circumstantial evidence is often referred to as the "blood of the martyrs," which recalls the words of Tertullian, an ancient Christian writer who wrote, "The blood of the martyrs is the seed of the church."[30] In other words, the church grew because the Apostles and the earliest followers died for what they believed. In other words, the conduct of the early Christians spoke volumes more than any writing or speech could.

Of all the acts of the Apostles, Paul's conversion stands out as particularly compelling and, therefore, worthy of note. Just as with the resurrection event itself, what set of facts could possibly explain the manner in which Paul acted? Paul had been strongly biased against accepting the truth of the Gospel—that Christ was God incarnate and was resurrected from the dead. Paul was well educated in Jewish law and custom. He viewed Jesus as a blasphemer and a scourge. He not only despised the followers of "The Way," he became preoccupied with eliminating this new sect that followed Christ. Yet, despite that predisposition, Paul not only accepted Jesus as his Lord and Savior, but he also devoted his entire remaining life to writing and speaking about the Gospel.

Recall also that Paul actively procured the right from Roman authorities to imprison, torture, and kill the early Christians. He was present at the stoning of Stephen, the Church's first martyr. If we fast forward a couple of years and observe his travels, missionary work, letters, and the persecution he suffered, we have to wonder what happened to change his behavior so radically. Why would anyone change his or her life so dramatically? If you lost interest in something about which you had been so zealous, would you turn 180 degrees and not only help the very people you maliciously persecuted, but become the most prominent and outspoken advocate for that group? And would you knowingly face the same type of persecution, mistreatment, and potential death that you had meted out? No. To me, it makes no sense at all. In Colson's own words—comparing the apostles with Nixon's men—"absolutely impossible."

I was becoming aware that the most likely explanation—the one that a reasonable, thinking person would find credible—for Paul's behavior was that he really did have a direct personal experience in which the resurrected Christ appeared to him. Paul's encounter with Jesus on the road to Damascus must have happened. Accepting that such a supernatural act happened may not be easy, but what other explanation makes any sense? What alternative normal or natural explanations might exist? It could not have been one or more of the other things that typically motivate people to act. Becoming a follower of Christ brought no power or prestige. Leadership positions with the early Christians didn't come with a big salary and bonus, a deferred compensation program, a supplemental retirement plan, paid parking, or a self-improvement allowance. In contrast, all the evidence reveals that Paul led a life of austerity, was unwelcome or ridiculed in public, and suffered imprisonment and death.

Having essentially conducted my own cross-examination of the known facts concerning the resurrection, not only did I find the truthfulness of the historical facts compelling, but now I was comfortable turning to other resources for corroboration. The New Testament accounts of the death and resurrection provide excellent supplemental or corroborating evidence. The Gospel narratives and Paul's letters also stand as important evidence for the resurrection. Paul said he saw Jesus after he died and was resurrected! He wrote:

> *For what I received I passed on as of first importance: that Christ died for our sins . . . that he was raised . . ., and that he appeared to Peter, and then to the Twelve. After that, He appeared to more than five hundred of the brothers at the same time, most of whom are still living. . . . Then he appeared to James, then to all the apostles, and last of all he appeared to me also . . . . (1 Corinthians 15:3-7)*

That fact alone, if true, would seem to carry enormous significance. Why would Paul record such an amazing, supernatural occurrence unless it actually happened?

Not only do Paul's writings add measurably to the historical record, but they also lead to an additional observation: to prove the Gospel writers, Paul, and the early Christians wrong would have been easy. If Christ had not been raised from the dead, someone could have pointed to the body or delivered the corpse. Christians never suggested that this resurrection was a private affair—not at all. Paul and the Gospel writers reported that Jesus had appeared to many after his death and resurrection, including "more than 500 of the brothers."

Notwithstanding these facts and the adversity with which the early church was met, I did not find any sources or historians that rejected the resurrection as an historical fact. Despite looking, I did not find any ancient writings in which the author points out, contends, or records that others (presumably non-Christians) testified that the story about the resurrection being repeated by the followers of Christ was simply untrue or otherwise wrong. And I found curious that atheists go to great lengths to try to explain away the empty tomb—the absence of a body. As I learned, the fact that Christ's body was missing is well documented or at least widely accepted. Thus, the tomb was empty.

Both the Roman and the Jewish authorities could have interviewed numerous individuals allegedly present at the time of the resurrection and obtained contradictory information— "sworn" testimony that the Christian account of the facts was not accurate. Yet, we have no record of any witnesses swearing emphatically that it never happened and no written reports of anyone saying, "I was there and Jesus never appeared, even though some of this cult's leaders say so." Moreover, many around ancient Palestine would have been motivated to do just that—to undermine this new band of brothers. Didn't the Jewish leaders or the Roman authorities, both of whom wanted to see this new religious sect disappear, have sufficient power to produce the body, produce a witness contradicting the reports, or even produce a person who would say whatever it was that the authorities wanted said, to end all the talk about Jesus being raised?

Book after book has been written on this topic of Christ's resurrection, with more appearing almost each year. That anything significantly new or different has been said or revealed is highly unlikely. For me though, and perhaps for many, arriving at a personal decision and a personal acceptance after appreciating rather than simply acknowledging the points and arguments was critical. To accept the words of scientists and believe that the earth rotates on its axis and revolves around the sun is one thing; to accept something as profound for your life as the recognition of God, salvation, and eternal life is quite another. For me, and I suspect for many, that form of acceptance requires something that moves the heart as well as the mind. Recognizing that the resurrection appeared to be true was an extraordinary step in my journey—as the saying goes; it appeared to be a game-changer.

Yet, for whatever reason, I failed (or refused) to make the ultimate commitment. Like the miles of a very long run, I continued on without reaching a finish line. Yet, it seemed to be in sight. I should be able to finish up this journey, but I started to wonder whether my reticence was because I really was unsure or because I was suppressing the truth, afraid of what an acceptance of Christ might require for my life.

Completing the Run: The NYC Marathon

Do you not know that in a race all the runners run, but only one gets the prize? Run in such a way as to get the prize.

—1 Corinthians 9:24 (NIV)

The marathon is based upon the legendary run that Pheidippides made after the battle of Marathon to advise the leaders of Athens that the Greeks had been victorious over the larger Persian army. After announcing, "Rejoice. We conquer!" he collapsed and died.

A race to commemorate Pheidippides's run was staged at the rebirth of the modern Olympics in 1896. Following Greek legend the race organizers determined that the distance from the plains of Marathon to Athens was 24.8 miles. The odd distance of 26.2 miles was the result of the King and Queen of England wishing to see the finish of the 1908 Olympic Marathon in London from their royal box. Distance was added to the race to accommodate their request, and ever since 1908, most marathons including Olympic marathons have adopted that distance as the official length of the modern marathon—twenty-six miles, three hundred eighty-five yards.

In most novice programs, the runners never run farther

than twenty miles before the marathon and usually have only one training run of that distance. Dan and I completed our one twenty-mile training run in the middle of October. Like many of the longer runs, the twenty-miler was not easy, but we finished. The weather was uncomfortably warm, and Dan started to get some modest cramping in his calves; but we finished. With that in the books, I was ready for what our running coaches call the taper, as I began to prepare mentally for marathon race day.

The taper is a two or three week period of cutting back training miles to allow the runner's body to recover from the weeks of training and prepare for the big day, that is, to recover, repair, and restore after twenty weeks of pounding. After the twenty-miler, the long Saturday runs decreased to twelve miles and then to eight the week before race day.

Dan and most of our other novice teammates were training for the Richmond Marathon a week later, but race day for me was running in the ING New York City Marathon. I was both apprehensive and excited.

Two of my law partners, Ray and Steve (who had run the Virginia Beach half-marathon when I had a few months earlier) were also running New York, so we made plans to enjoy some of the weekend together. I arrived on Friday and met up with them at the expo to pick up our official bibs, timing chips, and goodie bags. The expo was exhilarating. Excitement and anticipation are in the air—runners everywhere, booths of vendors, and everything about and for runners collected in a convention center. An enormous Nike store selling was selling ING NYC clothing and race-related and logoed merchandise. I bought my own souvenirs as well as shirts for Mike and Dan.

Manufacturers of gels and sports drinks, running gadgets, and sponsors of other races around the country as well as international destinations were there. I got particularly excited when I paused at a booth promoting the Edinburgh Marathon. Each spring I travel to Scotland to explore golf and its history. The individual manning the booth passed out brochures and encouraged the runners walking by to sign up for the May 2008 run that begins just below the historic castle in the capital of Scotland. I immediately realized that the date of the run was the same week I usually traveled to Scotland. It was meant to be! Maybe I'd run in Edinburgh. I spoke for a minute to the booth manager; he knew my friend back in East Lothian—what a small world. After a quick pizza and salad dinner, we headed to Madison Square Garden crowded with Baby Boomers for The Police reunion concert.

The next morning we met at Rockefeller Center for the start of the U.S. Olympic trials for the marathon to be held in Beijing in 2008. We followed the race up to Central Park, where the competitors would make four loops of a six-mile circuit. I didn't think watching people run around in the park was likely to be very interesting, so we walked to the finish line at Tavern on the Green and settled into some seats in the bleachers. It was the same finish line I hoped to cross the following day.

We were able to watch the runners come by and then followed them on a jumbo-tron as they headed around the park. What we didn't know at the time, and would not learn until that evening's news, was that one of the nation's top runners, Ryan Shay, collapsed and died near East 72nd Street during his first lap around Central Park about five miles into the race. Shock and sadness in the running world: "We have absolutely tragic news confirmed that Ryan Shay passed away today," said Mary Wittenberg, the CEO of New York Road Runners. This terrible event did not make me question whether I should attempt the run the next day. I was glad that Cheryl had not heard the news or was keeping her inevitable (and probably intensified) fears to herself.

We saw Ryan Hall win the qualifier, which sent him as well as the second and third place finishers to the Olympics. Ray, Steve, and I walked toward our Times Square hotels, stopping first for eggs and bacon at a Greek diner, and by two o'clock, we were seated for a matinee performance of *Les Miserables*. It was exceptional.

Afterwards, we found an Italian restaurant and enjoyed a typical, pre-race pasta dinner. A couple of glances around the room confirmed that we were likely to see most of the other restaurant patrons on the racecourse the next day.

The official start time for New York City marathon is 10:30 A.M., much later than most races. Getting to the start and waiting is part of the experience. Typical of other runners, I awoke at five and had my standard race-day breakfast: coffee and a banana and peanut butter on an English muffin. Then we caught a bus to Staten Island.

Due to the logistics of getting forty thousand people to the starting area, runners have to take early trains, buses, and ferries. When we arrived at Fort Wadsworth on Staten Island just below the Verrazano Narrows Bridge, we were directed to our "village" based on the color of our bibs. The start area is divided into a Green, Orange, and Blue villages. For almost three hours runners wait, worry, rest, eat, worry, talk about prior races, encourage new runners, meditate, attend religious services, and enjoy free coffee, bagels, and water. But most of all, they wait and prepare mentally for a very long run.

Another feature of the wait is the need to stay warm. The race is, after all, in November. Although the idea of a drop bag that will be delivered to the finish areas is a good one, the wait between the drop-off deadline and the start is long enough that runners typically wear throw-away clothes as well.

In addition to finding my village, I located my "pace team." I had decided I wanted to break the five-hour mark. With my typical pace of ten-and-a-half- to eleven-minute miles, the goal was not ridiculous. While I was at the expo, I ran into a booth of volunteers organizing and offering pace teams. I thought running with a group seeking a similar time might help me with my five-hour goal. I decided to run with the pace team that would finish in four hours and forty-five minutes or about eleven minutes a mile.

As the pace team, about forty strong, gathered to await start, I met a thirty-year-old woman from Washington State running her fourth marathon. What surprised me was her fuel belt in which she carried a number of items, including food, cell phone, camera, and a few bottles of water. I also met Alberto, an Italian-American, running his first marathon. Finally, we heard a cannon blast for the start of the men's open division, and twenty-one minutes later, I crossed the starting line to begin my marathon run.

As our 4:45 Pace Team walked from our gathering point to the start, we passed piles and piles of abandoned sleeping bags, winter jackets, blankets, and all forms of clothing used by the runners to stay warm during the three hour wait in the runners' villages. I learned that as soon as the race begins, Goodwill Industries shows up in force and collects these abandoned items. Obviously, this not only helps immeasurably to cleanup Ft. Wadsworth, but Goodwill can recycle the useable clothing and other items to those in need.

While this will sound like an exaggeration, it is not. No sooner had I crossed the starting line and begun an easy jog then I stepped on a balled-up sweatshirt at the entrance to the Verrazano Narrows Bridge—obviously shed by a runner who had kept it on to stay warm until the start.

When my right foot stepped on that sweatshirt ball, my ankle twisted hard, and I had some pain. I couldn't believe it. After eleven months, enormous progress, the weekend activities, and the three-hour wait, my journey would end ten yards from the start. I stopped. I cursed. I set my foot down, tested it, and waited for the pain. The ankle wasn't exactly normal, but the pain seemed to have already subsided substantially. I tried to jog lightly as hundreds of other runners passed me from behind, beginning their own journey through New York City's seven boroughs.

The ankle felt okay, so I picked up the pace a little and settled in next to Alberto, whom I had met while the pace team was gathering. Our leader, who carried a small 4:45 Pace Team sign on the end of a stick (and apparently planned to carry that sign for twenty-six miles) was just ahead. I was exhilarated! Here I was, running up the Verrazano Narrows Bridge in the first mile of the New York City Marathon. As I finished that mile and reached the center and highest point of the bridge, I could see Brooklyn straight ahead and the tall buildings of Manhattan in the distance. Wow, what a view! A beautiful morning! The sun was out, the air was clear and cool, and tugboats in the harbor were spraying water to celebrate the race start.

A large sign marked every mile, and next to the sign was a clock displaying the elapsed time. Because the clock started upon the firing of the race cannon and I took twenty-one minutes to get to the start line, I had to subtract twenty-one minutes for my time and pace. I was also wearing my Garmin Forerunner 305 GPS watch that allowed me to measure my pace, distance, running time, average pace, last lap pace, last lap time, and a multitude of other statistics, including the time of day, date, direction, and the calories I was burning. So as Alberto and I reached Mile 1, I touched the Lap button the GPS watch to record that we had completed one mile.

I glanced down at the watch's LED readout. It said 10:11. "Alberto," I said, "that mile was 10:11. A little fast." He agreed, sharing my concern that we had gone out too fast.

To run the marathon in 4:45, we had to average almost exactly eleven minutes per mile. We had just run the first mile almost a minute too fast. While perhaps it was way too early to panic, one of the most common mantras of experienced running coaches and most published running magazines is "Do not go out too fast." I knew that. I had heard it, read it and lived it. So I was somewhat distressed. If anything, experts will urge runners to go out slower than the average pace needed for the first few miles. We had already broken one of the Ten Commandments of running races.

Alberto and I shared a brief word of disappointment, but ran on. I felt great regardless. I was enormously excited as I glided downhill on the second half of the bridge with the entire course in front of me. I could still see the Manhattan skyline. Was I really going to run all the way to the Chrysler building!?

As we came to the end of the bridge, the horizon gave way to our first encounter with the New York City crowds. I touched my Garmin again to register the end of Mile 2. Somewhat horrified, I noticed that it read that we had completed the second mile at a pace of 9:10! I mentioned this to Alberto, who again wordlessly expressed some consternation. How could this be? I might have been the rankest amateur, but I was running with a "pace" team, lead by an experienced runner.

As I touched my GPS watch to set it for the next lap, I heard others nearby with similar watches that were issuing alert bells. I was shocked to see some women next to me stop and begin walking. I thought to myself, you must really not be in shape if you have to walk already. We have twenty-four miles to go. After a few more minutes or miles, I noticed other groups stopping at regular intervals and walking. Then I recalled that our daughters' French teacher, who was out there with me that first, chilly January morning when I attempted my first mile with the YMCA 10K training team, was experienced in a "walk-run" method, which features regular walking intervals to provide adequate rest to get the runner thorough the entire 26.2 miles. Former Olympic runner Jeff Galloway has probably prompted this approach most. All I could think was that no "real man" would try to run a marathon by walking any part of it. (I was even concerned that I was cheating because I had decided I would walk through the water stops when taking a drink.) After all, I had crossed the Verrazano Bridge and the first two miles of the race in an average pace of well under 10 minutes a mile. I was well on my way to conquering this race.

The crowds of race fans helped to deflect my thinking and lift my spirit. I will never forget the very first sign I saw as we came into Brooklyn. It was being held by a sixty-year old man and it read, "24 miles To Go—No Alternative!" You have to love New York.

Shortly after I saw that sign, the route took a left turn onto 92nd Street and an elderly woman shouted to me, "You're almost there." I couldn't help but smile. I had heard about the New York crowds, but I still couldn't believe the numbers and the enthusiasm. Race fans covered nearly every foot of the race on both sides of the street. I was only a couple of miles in, but my legs felt great, my energy was fine, and the crowd's enthusiasm helped carry me along.

Despite my best laid plans—and I could go on for some time about the lessons I learned on my own and from others related to relieving yourself as you prepare for the race start—I sensed a need to urinate. It wasn't severe, but since that was on my mind and not going away, I decided to relieve myself now and not waste the mental energy thinking and perhaps worrying about it for ten or twelve miles. Just as the race has mile-markers and clocks each mile, a race as large and as well run as the NYC Marathon also has water and sports drink available about every two miles. The stations are lines of tables with the drinks pre-poured and volunteers offering cups to runners. And, at every station is usually a bathroom or, more accurately, a Port-O-John. So I began to look for the next water station.

I took half a cup of water at Mile 3 and began to scope out the Port-O-Johns, pausing long enough to notice that we had run Mile 3 at a 10:45 pace. Better. I quickly spotted the johns, but just as quickly spotted a line of seven or eight women already waiting. I was not going to upset my time this early, so I decided I could wait.

About a mile later, I spotted a small park off to my right. Two policemen were on the sidewalk right next to the park entrance, so I thought relieving myself there probably wasn't a good idea until I noticed eight or ten guys using the park for that purpose and found my own tree. Not even the slightest glance or word from New York's finest. I'd see later how during a race like this, modesty goes right out the door.

By Mile 4, I had settled in pretty well. My bladder was no longer a distraction; the crowds were exhilarating. I disconnected from Alberto with my bathroom break, but I could see my 4:45 pace team not too far ahead, and soon I caught up with them. At Mile 5, I noticed our pace was 11:28. It was slower than the planned pace, but I figured that we still had to be ahead because of those fast early miles.

We ran through a variety of old, ethnic neighborhoods in Brooklyn. I could tell from the flags, the accents, the aromas, and the music as I went from Mexican to Polish to Italian neighborhoods. Some of the smells and sounds might have differed, but the enthusiasm of the people lining the streets was constant. I couldn't really understand why someone—never mind two million people—would spend a few hours standing around while overweight fifty-year old men jog by them. We weren't near any competitive runners; they had passed this spot an hour (or more) earlier. Why would spectators still be here to cheer on some purely recreational runners hoping to somehow finish a twenty-six-mile race? And at a 4:45 pace, no one is racing at all unless it's against oneself and the distance. But the crowds stayed and cheered.

Rock and other bands were set up sporadically along the route. I saw long extension cords pulling alternating current from a nearby church or commercial establishment powering amplifiers and boom boxes. People, especially children, reached their hands out for a high-five. On the route I regularly ran into private refreshment stations, where individuals offered orange slices, Gummy Bears, pretzels, water, and the like. I passed on all of these handouts, except one. My favorite surprise "give-away" by a thoughtful race fan was a wet wipe during the second half of the race. I gratefully took one so I could take some of the sweat and grit off my face, especially the salt gathering near my eyes.

I had a plan for staying hydrated, which our coaches and all running books routinely stress. If you speak to enough runners, you will hear an endless variety of recommendations about what and how often to drink. One thing that seemed universal was that if you were thirsty, you were already taking in too little fluid. With the number of runners crisscrossing one another, the mass of volunteers reaching out to offer cups of water, and the related change in the pace of those running nearby, runners need some art to successfully navigating the water stop.

One of the benefits of entering some running events during

training, especially a big half-marathon like Virginia Beach, is experiencing some of the challenges faced during the marathon itself. The water stop is one of those. Perhaps not surprisingly I found that too many runners stopped as soon as they reached the tables and the volunteers handing out water or sports drink, becoming obstacles blocking the tables. Not only had I decided to alternate the drinks I would take (Gatorade at one stop and water at the next), I also knew that the front of each stop would be for those seeking just water and that the group of tables and volunteers beyond would have the sports drink. So I would run through most of the stop and target the very back of the group of volunteers to try to avoid as many collisions as possible. Calling out what you want as you near a volunteer and try to make eye contact is also helpful. I would then walk (Heaven forbid!), because I found that I couldn't effectively drink water while trying to run. And then, on the road again.

Somewhere around the halfway point, I abandoned my Pace Team. I had become too frustrated by the push and pull of inconsistent pace—with some miles near ten-minute pace but others near a twelve-minute pace. I was concerned that this running style was not best for me or my objectives. Ultimately, I determined that being constantly preoccupied by this dilemma would not be good. I decided that it was best to get into my own pace. I continued to feel good. So far, so good.

The 59th Street or Queensboro Bridge is around the sixteen-mile mark. As I approached, some anxiety set in about this bridge. Not only were we well into the race, but a friend who had run the race mentioned that it was her least favorite part of the route. Also, our Pace Team leader had suggested that the group walk up this bridge if we were otherwise on pace. This seemed to confirm the fear my friend had unintentionally placed in me about the difficulty of this segment of the race. Looking back, I can confirm that the biggest hill on the course is the trek up the "Feelin' Groovy" bridge, and it proved to be a difficult climb. I took a couple of short walk breaks, as much of those running at my pace were doing, but continued to be on pace for a 4:45 marathon.

Coming off the 59th Street Bridge was another story. In fact, it was quite exhilarating. The crowds at and around the base of the bridge were among the most enthusiastic, welcoming us to Manhattan. And, the crowds were three and four deep! Amazing. After coming down the backside of the bridge, I entered my next to last borough, looped under the bridge, and then headed up First Avenue for a long run to the Bronx.

First Avenue was among the widest parts of the race. Not only had the runners separated and thinned by Mile 17, but First Avenue is a broad street. Sensing some fatigue, I gradually moved from the center of the avenue to the side where I knew the crowds would yell out my name and encouragement. (I had learned that many runners write their names on their bib or running shirt so the crowds could personalize their shouts of encouragement. I had "BRUCE" in large letters on my chest, just above my race bib.) Between Mile 17 and 18, PowerBar has a stop for runners to pick up a free gel. I used this opportunity to take a gel and to hook up my iPod.

I had carried my iPod Shuffle and earphones in the rear pocket of my running shorts pocket for 18 miles. I anticipated that the finish—the last five or six or so miles of the race—might be difficult, and I thought listening to some upbeat or inspirational music such as "Start Me Up" by the Rolling Stones, "On the Road Again" by Willie Nelson, or "Born to Run" by Bruce Springsteen might help me through the wall and during the tough, final miles. I made a very brief stop, glanced around for the iPod Nazi, downed a gel, and fixed my earphones, and I was on the road again. Despite these precautions, I still realized very soon that twenty-six miles is a very long way.

First Avenue heads uptown, and around Mile 19, the racecourse heads across the Harlem River on the Willis Avenue Bridge and enters the Bronx—the final borough. About halfway across this relatively short and flat bridge, I started to think that I might be running out of gas. I was getting tired. More accurately, my legs started to feel heavier.

As much as I hate to admit it, I walked for a couple of minutes as we crossed the bridge. The marathon's foray into the Bronx is brief—from just before Mile 20 to Mile 21. Nonetheless, this was the first time in three-plus hours that I realized finishing the race would not be easy. A large jumbotron was set up in the Bronx at a turn so runners could see themselves on TV. As I began to shuffle along, I had no interest in looking—I was beginning to realize that I was going to have some issues with just finishing. This thought was distressing. I walked a little more in the Bronx and then made my way back into Manhattan. After shuffling around Marcus Garvey Park, I turned onto 5th Avenue. I had passed the Mile 22 marker, but the going was getting hard.

What I probably didn't realize at the time was that I had "hit the wall," that proverbial runner's barrier where the legs just no longer want to do and barely can do whatever the mind beckons. "Hitting the wall," which many runners refer to as "bonking," is probably more physiological than anything else. Frank Shorter has said that the marathon may be the perfect distance to see what the human competitor can accomplish because of "the size of our gas tanks." What he means is that we are only able to store a certain amount of glycogen in our muscles. Glycogen fuels our running. Part of training for such a race is improving your body's ability to store and utilize that glycogen; but when all said and done, a person's "gas tank" really doesn't have enough to cover twenty-six miles.

Hitting the wall, then, is the bundle of physical symptoms resulting from the depletion of glycogen stores. I had reached this point but hoped to find some ability to push on farther nonetheless. Theoretically, the wall is why runners go to pasta dinners before a race or ingest a gel or "Gu" during the race. The goal is to fill one's tank to the max the night before and to anticipate the depletion of glycogen during the marathon.

I had taken a gel at Mile 19, but it did not appear to have had any impact. I was really tired and appeared to be fading. I had about four miles to go. I was going to do it. I was going to finish. I knew that, but I did not know how. This is why many say that the marathon is really two races in one—the first twenty miles and then the final 10K. It was certainly true for me. Up ahead, 5th Avenue rose gently; I could see hundreds of runners ahead. I could see where I needed to go.

I decided—right or wrong—to take a rest break at the next water stop. So, just before Mile Marker 23, I took a half of a cup of water, hit my Lap button on my GPS, and started a five-minute walk. I was going to take a "real" break and see if that would get me ready for the finish. After my brief walk, I started to run again, but my legs really weren't responding. I started to think about the need, or certainly the desire, to stop again. I really didn't have much interest in placing one foot in front of the other anymore.

Fifth Avenue is relatively flat but rises slightly uphill approaching 90th Street and the entrance to Central Park. After my five-minute "rest" I started to run again, but I was terribly exhausted. I had to run and walk the next two miles. To keep motivated, I would run three-quarters of a mile and then walk half of a mile; or I'd run half a mile and walk a half or a quarter of a mile. Up ahead, I finally saw the right hand turn into the park. From there, *only* about two and a half miles remained.

After some distressed walking and running, I was excited to enter Central Park. The crowds were particularly deep and encouraging. People would call out my name and shout—"Good job, Bruce!" or "Bruce, you are almost there!" I just couldn't believe it. These were wonderful people. How long had they been out there? The elite runners had run by over three hours ago! Marin Lel won the ING NYC Marathon that year with a time of 2:09:04, and Paula Radcliffe won the women's race with a time of 2:23:09. But here these incredible New Yorkers still stood and shouted encouragement more than two and a half hours later. But I was hurting. Despite the spirit of and cheers from the spectators, I really wanted to quit.

The route through the Park included some rolling hills. I shuffled up the hills as best I could and decided to let gravity pull me down. Around Mile 24 I noticed a camera up ahead on a slight upslope. Out of vanity (I didn't want to see photographs of me walking) and as a motivator, I ran down the hill and then up and under the camera. Then, I took a walk break. Thankfully, before long I was shuffling up a slight hill heading out of the Park to 59th Street at The Plaza Hotel. After that, I knew I was almost there—less than a mile to go! I looked at my watch and thought, "I can break 5 hours."

I turned right on Central Park South (59th Street) and headed for Columbus Circle. This segment, of course, was just the width of the Park. I could figure out some way to cover that distance, which had seemed like nothing during the few recreational runs I had "in the Park" during business trips to New York. People continued to line both sides of the raceway. I hurt. I could barely put one foot in front of the other. I started to run a quarter of a mile and walk a little. Run a quarter of a mile and walk a quarter of a mile. I recall running (or walking) close to a few race volunteers on 59th Street, who cheered me on. I felt that I was letting them down as I *walked* past them. Embarrassed, I struggled to pick the pace up to at least a jog.

Finally, I reached Columbus Circle. I knew what I had to do. I had walked this part of the route when we had watched the Olympic Trials the day before. Was it really only a day earlier? In my state it seemed like a month or a year earlier. The final quarter mile of the racecourse heads back into the Park from Central Park South with a right turn, down a small incline, and then a left turn onto the final approach. I let gravity help me down the slope and began to realize I really was going to do it. I looked at my watch again. Completing the run in 4:45 was a goal I dropped in the Bronx, but it looked like little was going to stop me from coming in less than five hours.

Now I was on the approach, an upslope to the finish line. The crowds were deep and enthusiastic. I knew the end was near. I

had to push on, just for another four hundred yards or so. I was
exhausted, but nothing hurt—no sharp pains, nausea, or cramps.
The final three hundred yards of the finish of the NYC Marathon
is up a small hill and then flat to the finish beside the iconic Tavern
on the Green restaurant. The bleachers I sat in the previous day
were almost on both sides of me. I was very close to the right side
of the course and, of course, close to the race fans there. They
cheered and called my name. It really was fun now. I glanced ahead
and saw the finish where Ryan Hall had become the first qualifier
for the Olympics. I had just about made it. And, incredibly, at all
times, as I tried to climb the final, modest incline, I felt a cramp
at the top of my knee, at the base of my left quadricep.

As much as it seems like a scene contrived for a book or movie,
I began to cramp up with a few hundred yards remaining. I had
run twenty-six miles without a hint of cramps of any kind and
now this! I stopped, tried to stretch a little, and off I went. I
cramped and stopped again. I actually laughed at the absurdity
of the moment. I was not upset, I only had three hundred yards
to go, and I knew I would make it somehow. Nearly holding on
to the iron rail crowd barrier to stable myself for a stretch, a few
race fans, who now were just a foot or two away, urged me on.
So I straightened up and tried again. Finally with two hundred
yards to go and with a shuffle more than a jog or run, I climbed
the final incline and saw the finish. I could not help but notice
the photographers just beyond the finish line, so I decided to try
a smile, which actually wasn't hard to do. I crossed under the ING
banner and across the electronic finish.

Four hundred miles away, Cheryl was watching Brooke, our
older daughter, compete in a tennis match for the William &
Mary club team. She had set up a laptop outside, and our niece
had helped her find a Wi-Fi connection. The NYRR provides an
opportunity for friends and family members to track a runner's
progress by registering on its website to receive updates during
the race in real time. Cheryl was concerned if not scared by the
prospects of her fifty-year-old, overweight husband trying to

run twenty-six miles. She had wondered if she should have come to New York "in case something happened." Brooke quickly reminded her if anything did "happen" to me during the race, the chances were infinitesimal that she would have been nearby at the time of any medical emergency. So, Cheryl posted up at the computer so she could see the tennis match as well as when I crossed the 10K point, the halfway mark, and various other points along the marathon route. Her sister Tina later reported to me, "the biggest smile came across her face when she was able to see that you had finished." I am sure Cheryl was happy, but I'm more convinced that she was also very relieved.

I had finished. My GPS watch said 4:57:28. I had beaten the five-hour mark, even if just barely. That day, I was one of 38,607, including Lance Armstrong and Katie Holmes (I only finished ahead of one of them) who crossed the finish line. All in all, I was very happy. In a matter of moments, volunteers placed a finisher's medal around my neck, another one took my photograph, and a third wrapped me with a "space blanket." I then shuffled along the path north toward Harlem and the UPS trucks with hundreds of fellow finishers. Other volunteers handed me water and a bag of recovery food items, including a bagel, an apple, and an energy bar. Trading hellos and congratulations with other runners, I continued to shuffle north and eventually picked up the bag I had checked with UPS back on Staten Island. After a few more crowded steps, a left hand turn and a brief walk west and up a path, I eventually exited the Park onto 8th Avenue and into the runner greeting areas. I made my way slowly, gingerly, but with a great sense of satisfaction, a medal around my neck and a space blanket wrapped around my body, down Broadway to my hotel in Times Square.

CHAPTER 12

HITTING THE WALL—AGAIN

The reason I fell is because I am and was
very inexperienced in running in a pack.

—Mary Decker

"Contentment." That's your secret. I'm 24 and I've never known it.
I'm forever in pursuit and don't even know
what it is I'm chasing ... Aubrey, old chap, I'm scared.

—Harold Abrahams (from *Chariots of Fire*)

I had finished the New York City Marathon, and, I have to admit,
I was very pleased with the accomplishment. I wrote significant
portions of this memoir training for it and worked through many
of the thoughts set out here on my morning runs alone and Saturday training team runs. Unfortunately, I still wasn't sure what
I believed. Colson's proof of the resurrection was compelling,
yet some doubts persisted. I still hadn't finished that journey.

I am embarrassed to admit that I had the idea of going to St.
Patrick's Cathedral and making a new commitment to Christ the
day before the race believing that renewed faith would help get
me to the finish line. It seemed like a perfect way to exploit the
metaphor of this memoir. Apparently, I was thinking too much
about the movie version of this book. I may have struggled up 5th
Avenue during the race, but I missed my pre-race appointment
at St. Patrick's.

Shortly after the marathon, Carl called to congratulate me, and we decided to meet for a lunch or dinner soon. When we got together, he was kind to compliment me on the accomplishment of completing the marathon. I had indeed come a very long way in eleven months; but as he continued to stress what a feat it was, I finally said, "If I could do it, you certainly can." Those were almost the exact words my college roommate Randy had said to me thirty years earlier. Carl begged off just as I once did, but I persisted. He had been running three or four miles fairly regularly, and I explained how he was farther along than I was when I got started. Sometime during that celebratory lunch, I convinced him to run a half-marathon in Williamsburg with my daughter Brooke and me, a race that was three or four months off.

A few days later, a professional situation developed that shook almost every foundation in my life. Because of an omission I made, I became worried that most of what I had worked for might slip away very quickly. The issue had the potential, at least I thought, to bring me severe criticism, if not disgrace. The potential impact on my family and how my family and friends might see me in the future caused concern to build. My mind raced with the possible dire consequences. I reached near desperation one day as I drove west across Virginia from Richmond and over Afton Mountain. I imagined a fall from grace and could see and play out the embarrassment. I dreaded the reaction of friends, family, and colleagues and wondered if this would wreck my financial security. Near panic started setting in.

Without the sort of intentional, rational process I would undertake to solve a problem, I found myself calling out to God without worrying about the nuances of the apologetics I had been studying. More than anything else, I urgently wanted to make a bargain with God. "If I can only get through this situation..." I began to think.

As much as I wanted God to answer my prayers and cut a deal with me, I was just as urgently overtaken by disgust. I was angry about the mistakes that had made this situation possible, and I was disgusted that I was now trying to dodge my personal responsibility and find a divine cure—trying to obtain an undeserved "Get Out of Jail Free" card.

Something Tim Keller said hit me. I had focused far too much on advancing my personal influence, importance, prestige, and wealth. Wasn't this part of what my brother observed many years earlier that had kept us apart? I had put my trust, my hope, and presumably my search for meaning in a chase for greater recognition and more material things rather than deeper relationships. If Keller was right, those were the things I worshipped. I had placed my trust and hope in personal achievement, holding onto those things as my idols, the gods who would save me. And, if Keller was right, to do that was to sin. Even the lawyer in me couldn't come up with a rebuttal. At that point, I stopped looking to negotiate a deal with God. Instead, I asked God for forgiveness and for guidance.

As it turned out, the professional issue that had so shaken my world was resolved. The worst never happened. My fears were not realized. I was not disgraced. The problem was not as crucial or desperate as I imagined. Yet, the glimpse into my soul was very real. The recognition of where I had placed my trust and the corresponding recognition of sin was real, critical, and desperate. Somewhat like Jacob Marley, I had a glimpse of the abyss, but it appeared I also had the chance to learn from the encounter.

But in this crisis had I just answered all my questions? Had I, without thinking, both reached a conclusion about God and responded to it? What did this seemingly involuntary or instinctive cry for God mean amidst my questions and doubt? And hadn't I just experienced a taste of redemptive grace—something I was beginning to understand better as I proceeded on my journey?

CHAPTER 13

THE RUN: BEGINNING AGAIN

Those who run after other gods will suffer more and more.

—Psalm 16:4 (NIV)

A week after the marathon but prior to my road trip over Afton Mountain, I met Dan at the start line for the Richmond Marathon. He was surprised (I was surprised) that six days after the NYC Marathon, I would be trying to run another twenty-six miles.

We gathered for a training team (MTT) photograph on Main Street and then headed two blocks up the hill to find our way to the start line on Broad Street. We used the Port-a-Johns and waited nervously around the start area. Shortly before the race began, my good friend and law partner, Mike, stepped into our corral. "I'm not feeling well," he said, "can I run with you?" I said, "Of course." Mike had run three or four of the prior Richmond marathons and was a stronger runner with the flu than I was healthy.

I had decided to try to run in the Richmond Marathon because Dan and I had trained together so long that I wanted to run with him as far as I could. I figured I could probably do half the race. During the week after New York and leading up to the race in Richmond, I had an abundance of energy. I felt like I could run at least half of the upcoming marathon. I looked at the course map and concluded that if I could make it 16 miles, I would be fairly close to the finish. I could leave Dan, walk downtown, take a shower at my office, and then meet Dan at the finish. Most of this actually went as planned.

Mile 16 at Richmond is at the north end of the Lee Bridge. Although the marathon route uses this bridge to pass over a beautiful stretch of the James River, the mile across the river may be the most unpleasant part of that race. Not only does it come at a time when glycogen stores are getting short, but the bridge actually is uphill and exposed to the wind. Nonetheless, I made it across. We stopped at the sixteen-mile marker and wished Dan good luck as his cousin picked him up for the last ten miles. Mike and I walked a half of a mile to the point where the racecourse turns west up Main Street. This is the spot at which we were to head east to the finish area downtown. Just when I was ready to head in that direction Mike encouraged me, "We've come this far, do you want to finish?" So, with little contemplation, Mike and I turned west and headed out for the race's final ten miles.

It was not easy, and it wasn't long before I mentioned to Mike that I'd have to walk a little. So, for the final nine miles or so, Mike stayed with me, walking some and running some until we completed the 26.2 miles. In many respects it became agonizingly difficult, but we would set a short-term goal, conquer that, and then set another. I would say, "Let's run the next three quarters of a mile and then walk the last quarter," or we'd walk half a mile and then run a mile. Then maybe we'd do half of a mile running and half of a mile walking. One race photograph has the two of us smiling at the camera because we knew we had been caught walking, which for both of us was a strike against our ego. We did this until we reached the final left-hand turn onto Cary Street and then down the hill to the finish line at The James Center. I didn't beat five hours, but I had finished my second 26.2 miles in six days. (I cannot imagine the odds I might have gotten in Las Vegas or from the British bookies if I had suggested running two marathons within six days as the basis for a wager eleven months earlier.)

Shortly after the New York and Richmond marathons came the holiday season with Thanksgiving and then Christmas. I had lost weight down to a low of 218 pounds, forty-three pounds from my highest weight. Unfortunately, I was too pleased with my accomplishments, ate too indiscriminately, and slacked off with my exercise, missing many of my otherwise regular runs. I knew I needed to get back to morning runs and long weekend runs. My running buddy Dan having a minor medical procedure that kept him, and me to some extent, off the streets until January 1 sure didn't help. Without an MTT run to go to each Saturday I needed another New Year's resolution. In retrospect, I had made that already; I had committed to run the Edinburgh Marathon in May.

Dan recovered quickly from his operation and announced that he would be running all of my long training runs with me as I prepared for Edinburgh. We agreed to meet each Saturday morning and get in a long run. We got a good start after New Year's. Each week we would alternate between meeting downtown in the Fan District near Dan's house and at the Huguenot Bridge Starbucks, closer to my house. In an effort to keep up our fitness, we decided we would run ten to thirteen miles each Saturday. I noted how ridiculous that would have seemed a year earlier, going out and essentially running a half-marathon every weekend. But we could and often did do that. I had made some real progress.

We would run through and around downtown along many routes similar to the MTT ones. From Starbucks, we would run a figure eight that would take us through the hills of the University of Richmond, south across the Bridge, and then east, downriver along the James River. Sometimes, probably because it may be the prettiest run in Richmond, we would just head down the river for the entire ten to twelve mile run. Before long, the end of February had come, and we were headed to Williamsburg to run the Colonial Half-Marathon. This was the race I had convinced my friend Carl to run with us, but I wasn't certain that this day was going to come.

While Carl had run two to four miles fairly regularly, he had trouble getting the training in comfortably to prepare for this race. I had created a program for him of running three or four times a week with an increasingly longer weekend long run that I based off of the 10K and the MTT programs I had done. (In retrospect, I am not sure why I thought I was in a position to advise Carl about running—probably overconfidence occasioned by what I considered a remarkable accomplishment.)

Initially, the race seemed to be going fine, but then I received signals suggesting that Carl was struggling. He doubted his ability to run the half-marathon. Three weeks before the race, Carl emailed me:

> By the way, had a challenging run yesterday. Did only 4.25 miles. . .
> 10:45/mile pace and was very tired afterwards . . . discouraging.
> Travelling Tues-Wed and expect I will only be able to run on Monday,
> Thursday morning and Friday . . . would love your advice because I
> just don't see how I can go more than six to eight miles max.

Then, with two weeks to go before the race, Carl emailed me again:

> Went out for a four miler today and barely made 1.5 miles and that
> was at an 11 min/mile plus pace. I didn't run yesterday but still feel
> Saturday's 10 miler. I feel sluggish and frankly tired of running.
> Normally, doing 4 or 5 miles is good. I feel like I pushed myself but
> without overdoing it. I think I simply do not enjoy running more
> than 5 or 6 miles. I have done two 8 milers and struggled. The ten
> miler killed me and the thought of running 2.5 hours even factoring
> in how much I would enjoy the pleasure of your daughter's and your
> company is something I am now beginning to dread. In the end, I think
> I am a 5 or 10k runner and not a marathoner stud like you. Even if I
> wanted to keep pushing myself, I am not driven to run a marathon
> like you. I just want to stay in shape and this is too much for me.
>
> Let me know what you want me to do. 1) Given that I cannot see
> myself running anywhere near 13 miles on 2/22, if you want to spend
> your time with your daughter exclusively, that is ok. Maybe we can
> schedule another type of family get together. 2) If you want me to come

*up to Richmond that weekend to buy you all dinner and then let you
go to W'Burg without me, I can do that as well. 3) If you want me
to buy dinner and then run 5 or 6 miles and then laugh at me at the
end, I can do that as well.*

*I am sorry that I am not a stud like you but I tried. I just don't
have it in me and in the end, don't enjoy running that far. Let me
know what you want to do.*

As if I had become Bart Yasso or Jeff Galloway, I explained to
him that running in the middle of the day—when the weather was
sunny and 80 degrees, after skipping breakfast, failing to hydrate,
and not planning any water stops, might make a nine-mile run
rather challenging, if not unreasonably difficult. I eventually
figured out an excuse to get up to Northern Virginia, spend a
Friday night at Carl's house, and go for a long run with him the
next day. We had the obligatory English muffin with peanut butter
and a banana breakfast; then we headed out for what I hoped
would be a successful eight-mile run. I wore a fuel belt and a GPS
watch. The morning was pleasant, neither cool nor warm. Carl and
I always have much to discuss, so we had plenty of conversation.
At the four-mile point, we shared most of the water I had carried;
then we turned around and headed back toward his home on
one of Northern Virginia's rails-to-trails pathways. We finished
without any problems. Carl noted how much easier it had been
than he expected. I hoped this would help curb his doubts and
get him back on track for a successful half-marathon.

The night before the Williamsburg race, Carl came to Richmond.
We went out with Cheryl, Dan and his wife, and some other friends
for a traditional, pre-race pasta dinner. I say "traditional" because
every race of any consequence hosts a pasta dinner the night
before the race. The purpose was to carb-load, trying to maximize
the glycogen stored in our muscles. I learned that this was much
more relevant in the marathon than shorter races because our
muscles generally can store adequate energy for a race less than
eighteen miles. Thus, while probably unnecessary and barely
useful, pasta dinners preserve a running tradition and, more
importantly, are great fun.

With a midday race start, we drove the hour down to Williamsburg and met up with my daughter Brooke and her roommate, Anna (who is Randy's—my old college roommate's—daughter. Randy is the one with whom I had run my first marathon thirty years earlier). Knowing this was a big race for Carl, who had never gone thirteen miles, some of Brooke and Anna's friends at the college came out to cheer us on near the start. They had even prepared some posters that read "Meyer [as in Carl Meyer] on Fire"—hilarious. We had some good laughs and took some great photographs.

The Colonial Half doesn't have a large field, but those who show up are generally fast. The finish line closes two and a half hours after the race starts, so slower runners may not arrive in time for an "official" finish. We all got started just fine as the route headed out toward Colonial Williamsburg, passed by the Golden Horseshoe Golf Course, and then went out on the Country Road, a heavily wooded, little used road that rolls its way east toward Busch Gardens and the Kingsmill Resort. The only house along the way (and the site of my twentieth and thirtieth college reunions) is where local recording artist Bruce Hornsby lives.

Even with a few unplanned bathroom stops, everyone seemed to be doing fine. We ran as a group and maintained a pace that allowed everyone to talk comfortably. Brooke and Anna were very fit, such that from time to time they would run up and then back to visit with us. This was particularly enjoyable as everyone naturally took time to run and chat with everyone else in our little pack.

The race route was mostly out and back, so as we approached Mile 4 or 5 the real runners—college athletes keeping a five-minute-per-mile pace—were coming back toward us. Although a little disconcerted that they had completed more than twice the distance we had in the same amount of time, we were mostly impressed, and we clapped for them as they came by. At the halfway point we picked up some water and Gatorade. Everyone seemed in good shape for the run back to campus. We were clearly some of the slower runners but certainly not the last. With two or three miles to go, everyone still seemed to be doing fine and figured that we all would finish. A few moments later we passed a policeman stationed for traffic control and heard him speak into his radio, "I just have a few remaining stragglers here." We feigned outrage at the comment, laughed and moved on.

The Colonial Half-Marathon finishes in W&M Hall, the ten-thousand-seat arena where Carl and I saw many rock concerts and basketball games in the late 1970s and where the Tribe still plays basketball. This allowed friends and family to watch runners as they come into the Hall for their finish. With about a mile to go, we headed back onto to the campus as the race route led us to the Hall for the finish. I looked at my GPS watch and mentioned to Dan that it didn't look like we would meet the race cutoff of two hours and thirty minutes—but no bother, we would still all finish, we just might not have that dramatic finish of entering W&M Hall and crossing the line. Carl overheard this and, perhaps because he thought he was dragging us down, he immediately picked up the pace and continued to accelerate. Everyone followed along as we passed Crim Dell and ran through the Lodges. The pace was vigorous.

With about five hundred yards to go, we turned left and headed up a small incline, passing Yates Hall (my freshmen dorm) on the left, toward the W & M Hall. That's when Carl found still another gear and pushed us even faster. Despite picking up my own pace, I found I was falling behind, so I had to accelerate even more. Because of this unexpected activity, I barely saw Cheryl and Amy cheering us on outside the Hall as I finally caught up to the group. Carl and I led the group around the back of the Hall and, turning right into the Hall, crossed the finish line at exactly 2:30:00. It would take me six months to work out the modest strain I suffered to my upper hamstring during that last four-hundred-meter dash, but helping Carl to complete the race was more than worth it.

Shortly after the race in Williamsburg, I almost ran into—

literally—an acquaintance in the early morning as he walked out to get his newspaper. He lived about halfway between my home and my office in downtown Richmond, and I was taking one of my favorite runs as part of my mid-week longish runs, still trying to prepare for Edinburgh. Most marathon training programs incorporate an increasingly long mid-week run as the Saturday long run lengthens. During my novice year and while training for my first marathon, the Wednesday run increased to ten miles the month or so before the actual race day. Training for my spring race in Scotland, I tried to run a fairly long mid-week race as part of my conditioning. One day, I was thinking about how early I had to get up to run ten miles on a Wednesday and still get to work at a reasonable our when I thought, why don't I run to work? We have a good shower/locker room there, and if I brought clothes the day before, I could very easily get ready for work after running downtown from home.

I figured that it was 11 or 12 miles from my home to my office, so one morning I headed out around 5:30 A.M. I was very eager to see how this run would go. I had plotted a route that avoided the few busy streets between our house and downtown. That February morning was completely dark as I left our neighborhood. I took the dirt path over to Moreland Road and hung a left, heading north passing Collegiate School on my right. Then I went right into and through Sleepy Hollow and then left to Parham Road. Usually quite busy, Parham had traffic, but it was intermittent at 6 A.M. as I darted across and entered a subdivision heading east, up a short hill, and then right onto Ridge Road. Although this, too, is a fairly busy road, it was also very still at that time as only a couple of cars passed me during the five minutes I needed to return to quieter, neighborhood roads.

Running down the gentle slope of Ridge Road, the broad sky appeared for the first time as I escaped the canopy of leaves from the tree-lined streets predominant in neighborhoods through which I had just come. Now, I was looking due east—exactly where I was heading, toward downtown. Glancing up, the sky was clear and star-filled, dark behind, deep blue above, with a slowly developing red and orange glow at the horizon as the sun began to rise in the distance. I marveled at the beauty and the solitude for a moment. The only sound was my footfalls and the voice of Tim Keller in my ears as I listened to a new podcast.

My route then took me through neighborhoods that border the west side of the University of Richmond. The overall elevation continued to slope gently downward as I entered the Westhampton Campus of the University, formerly the women's college. Still deathly quiet, I ran by the women's field hockey/lacrosse turf field, between dormitories, and down a steeper hill—still not a soul to be seen. At the bottom of this hill, the lowest point at the University, I made a short right on a footpath onto the road that marked the north edge of the Country Club of Virginia. The road is very remote and dotted with a few homes overlooking the golf course. Due to the vegetation, the sky darkened and then disappeared back under a thick canopy of tree branches and leaves. After climbing a steep but short hill, the road flattens, and that is where I "ran into" my friend at his mailbox.

After a quick exchange of words, I headed east again and started the toughest part of the run. Climbing steeply for a good half mile, I finally reached Three Chopt Road, which is fairly busy, but again, at 6:30 A.M., still pretty quiet. After crossing I made a right at St. Bridget's Catholic Church and then two hundred yards later a left onto Grove, which I would be able to take straight down to the business center of Richmond. I touched my Garmin Lap button as it beeped at mile six of the run. I stopped, pulled the water bottle from my fuel belt, and drank some Gatorade. I felt great. The morning was clear and cool, about 45 degrees. The run was incredibly peaceful and just beautiful.

Grove Avenue is one of the prettier residential streets that fan out from downtown. Our MTT had logged many miles on this avenue because of its paved sidewalks and better width. It is one of the safer of the main arteries. Energized by the morning and completing the first half of the run, I put my water bottle back into the holder at the small of my back and picked up the pace. To my immediate right, I noticed some activity picking up at St. Catherine's, a private school for girls, and early morning commuters coming out of the Starbucks at Libbie and Grove— one of Richmond's small, but special, retail corners. In a very gentle, barely perceptible way, Grove Avenue runs downhill toward the city. As I pushed east, the volume of traffic increased substantially, though it still was not hectic.

I alternated between the sidewalks and the shoulder but had no problem being too close to oncoming vehicles. On my left, I passed Temple Beth-El and reached a crossing guard at St. Benedict Elementary School as the first students began to arrive. Before I realized it, the Virginia Museum of Fine Arts was on my left, and The Boulevard was directly in front of me. Pausing at the light for the first time since reaching Grove, I darted across as the traffic permitted, then stopped again and drank another three or four ounces of Gatorade. Now refreshed for the final push, I again headed east down Grove toward my office.

I felt fine, and I was enjoying the ever-changing light and activity. As the volume of vehicles, pedestrians, and ambient noise all rose, I experienced the day as it gradually awoke. The final three miles were much like the last three. A fairly flat run took me through two- and three-story detached but closely built homes typical of the Fan District. Soon the road dead-ended into the campus of Virginia Commonwealth University. After a few hundred yards, I came out on the other side and into Monroe Park. Crossing diagonally through the park, I had to wait for the light to cross Belvedere because commuter traffic was now vigorous. I turned onto Main Street, running against the traffic on this one-way street that heads west out of the downtown area.

Heading up a slight incline, I passed the historic Jefferson Hotel on my left, then the Richmond Public Library, and then from there, down the hill from 2nd Street into the busy business district. By then, people and cars were everywhere. The quiet of the early hours was long gone. The city was alive and gaining volume with every step. At 10th Street I had one more turn, dodging people and vehicles I headed right for two blocks and I arrived at the Riverfront Towers. I touched my GPS watch—12.1 miles; 2 hours, 4 minutes—very satisfying. I finished the last from my water bottle, made my way to the showers, and was at my desk by 8:10. I would repeat this run many times as I continued on my journey; and each time I finished I would note that this was probably "my favorite run."

Committing to run a spring marathon (the Edinburgh Marathon was at the end of May) means that runners must put in a lot of miles in the winter, which entails a lot of running in the cold. Richmond is in the South, but the temperature still gets into the teens many mornings in January and February. A year earlier, I had started in the winter, but that was mostly on a treadmill; and I was not going out for much more than two or three miles. As the weather turned after the New York and Richmond marathons, I had to learn to run in the cold.

Many mornings when I began I wasn't sure of what to wear. Sometimes on a four-mile run, I would be burning up after just a mile or two. On other mornings my hands and ears were uncomfortably cold. Eventually, after weeks of trial and error, I would check the local weather during my wake-up cup of coffee or two. Then, once I knew the temperature, I knew which weight of running shirt or shirts I would need and what to have on my legs to stay reasonably warm. Perhaps most important to me, to keep me out on the streets and resisting the urge to give up because "it's just too cold," was covering my hands and ears on the coldest mornings.

The coldest morning I ever tried to run was in Baltimore in February. My discipline about getting my weekly runs in was pretty good. I was at a hotel near the Inner Harbor, so I headed out in running pants, two layers of tops, gloves and a headband. The temperature was 17 degrees, but running along the harbor at 6 A.M. with a fair wind made conditions formidable. I didn't have to worry about car traffic; but after the first mile, I was not warming up. The breeze seemed to pick up moisture from the harbor and make the air almost hurt as it met the bare skin of my face. Rarely had I been so cold and unable to get comfortable.

After the second mile I noticed that even the warmest part of my body began to ache with a biting cold—this did not seem good. After 2.3 miles, I spotted my hotel just off the harbor and turned toward the Marriott sign, which was probably only a quarter of a mile away. I had had enough. I knew that this was not a run I was going to pursue farther.

As I continued to train for the Edinburgh Marathon, I received weekly emails about the race, including training tips, race day logistics, charity donation opportunities, and human-interest stories. One item I found particularly interesting was the race sponsor's suggested training schedule, which set out the number of *minutes* to be run each day as opposed to the number of *miles*. The 10K and marathon training programs I had seen had all been based on the number of miles to be run each day. Many, particularly recreational runners like me, find some benefits to focusing on minutes rather than miles. Another curious tidbit that I picked up, which may help if conversing with a running friend in the U.K., is that when discussing the best time you've ever had in a particular race—it's a PB ("personal best") in the U.K. and not a PR ("personal record") as it is in the U.S.

As May approached, we began to stretch our Saturday runs to fourteen and then sixteen miles, and we planned to go even farther.

For me, the toughest aspect of training for a marathon is the eighteen- or twenty-mile runs. I don't enjoy them. They are really hard work. When I acknowledge this to some, they often ask, "Why run twenty-six miles if eighteen or twenty are so difficult?" I explain that I do it to prepare mentally for the day that I step up to the starting line, with hundreds or thousands of other runners and a race atmosphere with cheering fans and waving banners. The first eighteen or twenty miles can be both challenging and fun. After that it's pure effort, mostly mental, to get one's body to cover those last six miles or so. Unfortunately, I always seem to "hit the wall." I have never had an easy time of finishing that last portion of a 26.2-mile race.

Running far is also much easier when the run is a "supported"—meaning there are SAGs ("snacks and gear") at various intervals during the run. The race can be even "easier" (a relative term) with the right race environment and "free" T-shirt.

I needed to get in at least one twenty-mile run before Edinburgh, and conveniently, the Charlottesville Marathon was being held four weeks before Edinburgh. I convinced Dan that we should use the Charlottesville race as a training run, because the race environment and the support makes such a long run much easier than trying to tackle it all on our own.

The morning of the Charlottesville Marathon was perfect weather—clear, sunny, and cool. The run left from the downtown mall area, passed through the University of Virginia campus, and headed out of town into rolling hills and horse country. This early run was beautiful as the dogwoods, daffodils, and many wildflowers were in bloom. The route rolled through the countryside, and then, after approximately six miles, we had to climb a fairly severe hill. For a moment, near that hill's summit, the thought of turning around with those competing in the half-marathon sounded like a good idea. Although tempted, we continued.

After a few more miles we caught up with two women runners from Philadelphia and fell into their pace, which was about the same as ours. We talked and ran with them for about four miles. As we all approached a SAG around Mile 18, I noticed that my energy was starting to fade. The women met up with their husbands at this SAG. As we took our sports drink, we bid the "Phillies" goodbye.

Even after finishing our hydration stop, I walked a little farther to extend the rest and then told Dan to go on without me. He seemed to feel good, and I wanted him to have the best race possible. At this point, the race route circled back and we now headed down that severe hill we climbed earlier. As I picked up running again and eased down the hill, I could see the route ahead as it led right and then uphill for what looked like forever. The course turned out to be three continuous miles of climbing, which after running twenty miles, might as well have been forever. I could not do it. In my mind I had completed my twenty-mile training run. With a little running interspersed I walked those three miles uphill. With a mile or two to go, I walked and ran my way to the finish. Dan came in about fifteen minutes before me. The hills had attacked him as well, leaving Dan with serious cramping in his calves and giving him a self-ascribed nickname— "gramps with cramps."

A month after our "twenty-miler" in Charlottesville, I lined up with over 11,000 others just below the historic Edinburgh Castle on Princes Street. The night before, I had pasta and marinara sauce at my hotel and then retired to my room to prepare for the race the next day. As recommended by many running experts, I attended to my pre-race organization rituals. I pinned my bib on the shirt I planned to wear the next day and laid out all of my other race items the night before. I got to bed at a decent time and rose with my alarm.

Outside my hotel I caught a bus that I had scoped out the day before, and before I knew it, I was at the start area with 11,000 of my new best friends. The day was breezy, cloudy and cold with moisture present and rain threatening—in other words, typical Scotland weather. I wore a black trash bag over my running shirt and shorts. I had learned this trick from one of my new running friends. The plastic trash bag is light and disposable, and it does a great job temporarily fending off the wind and preserving warmth as you wait for a race's start. It is also easy to run the first couple of miles with the trash bag on while you warm up. The race was about to begin, and I was eager to shed my black bag and get started.

We spilled downhill and ran past Holyrood Palace, the historic home of the royal family of Scotland. Before clinging to the south coast of the Firth of Forth, the route turned back toward

the seaport town of Leith until it reached the Firth. From there
the race followed the shore as it headed east along A-198, passing
through Musselburgh, Prestonpans, Cockenzie and Port Seton
as it tried to stretch all the way to Aberlady and Gullane Hill. As
an amateur golf historian, I knew that this run traced much of
the historic march of the game in its earliest years in the place
of its birth.

Golf as we know it got much of its start below Edinburgh
Castle at Bruntsfield and on the nearby links at Leith. Later, the
earliest clubs moved east seeking better and less-crowded public
space. Like the marathon route, these clubs led by the oldest,
the Honorable Company of Edinburgh Golfers, headed east in
1837 and set up operations at Musselburgh. At Musselburgh the
race arrives at Mile 10 (and later, finishes on a racetrack that
surrounds the historic golf course). This town serves as the first
rally point for the relay part of the marathon, which features
teams of runners where each team member runs a segment of the
race, typically to raise money for a charity. Again, like the course
of the race, the Honorable Company moved farther east at the
end of the nineteenth century, settling at Muirfield in Gullane
just two miles beyond the marathon turnaround point at Mile 18.

Fortunately the Edinburgh route does not return back to the
historic city—that would require a severe uphill run at the finish.
Rather, the marathon course finishes on a horse racetrack at
Musselburgh, which features the oldest continually used golf
course within its infield—and the one used by the Edinburgh
golf clubs relocating east of the city.

Making the turn at Mile 18, I felt pretty good, but could sense I
was running low on energy. A mile later, I stopped to walk a little
for the first time. From there I continued to walk and run the
next few miles. I became a bit discouraged because as I looked at
my watch, I concluded that my pace was now too slow to finish
within my five-hour goal. With a little less than three miles to go,
I overheard a woman who was coaching some friends say, "We're
right on pace to finish within five hours. C'mon, we can do it."

What?! Could I really break five hours? I looked at my GPS watch and did some quick calculations. Yes, maybe I could.

The next two or three miles were among the hardest I had ever run. Long ago I had hit the wall. I was shot, totally depleted, having used up all stores of glycogen, and I just wanted to walk my way to the finish. Actually, I wanted to sit down right then and there and have a cold drink and a warm shuttle to my hotel. Yet, something kept me going. My pace was probably 11½ or 12 minutes a mile or perhaps even slower, but I tried to put one foot in front of the other. The women who had unknowingly inspired me fell off, but with a mile to go, I figured if I could run it in about twelve minutes, I could break five hours. I pushed on, but every time I recommitted to pick up the pace, something within urged me almost immediately to rest. I just wanted to stop. I wanted to get off my feet. I wanted to quit. Finally, not too far ahead, I saw the stadium and the white fence of the horse track. "C'mon!" I said to myself, "It's not far now."

The race marshals led me through an opening through the fencing to permit the runners to finish in front of their friends and family on the track below the stadium seating. I looked up, which itself was not easy as I had been looking down at my feet and trying to summon enough strength to shuffle a little farther. I had about three hundred yards to go. I was not fully conscious but tried to keep my legs moving. I continued to glance at my watch. It would be close. Just a few more yards I told myself. And then, finally, I crossed the finish line. My watch said 4 hours, 59 minutes and 22 seconds.

After I crossed the finish, I wanted to sit down but knew I should not. At the same time, I sensed that I might pass out. I had to work hard to both keep myself vertical and alert. I was given my finisher's medal and a bottle of water. I decided just to walk slowly to the bag-check area where I could do one of my favorite things—put on a clean, cotton T-shirt. I was successful in that modest endeavor, and, as I began to think about it, in completing another very long run.

CHAPTER 14

THE RACE: IN PURSUIT

*You gotta have confidence. The question is, what are you putting
your confidence in: Your own ability? And what do you believe
about your ability? Do you believe you've done something to
deserve it? Or is it a gift? I believe I have a gift from God.*

—Ryan Hall

Not only had I gone from an inability to run even a mile to
completing the 26.2 miles of the New York City Marathon
eleven months later, but over the course of two years, I also completed marathons in Richmond, Charlottesville, Edinburgh, and
Richmond again. My spiritual journey had also gone far but had
not yet reached the finish line. I seemed to be having as much
trouble trying to determine what I believed as I did trying to finish each of my marathons. On perhaps life's most important
question, I had examined a significant body of evidence and had
studied most of the traditional arguments. Not only did much of
the evidence and many of the arguments make sense, but I also
found both to be persuasive. And some of them I found compelling. I had been humbled by the recognition of my own egotism.
I had, so to speak, "hit the wall." Yet I resisted any real acceptance
of the truth of the Gospel.

Maybe I still was looking for my own Damascus Road (the place
of Christ's appearance to the apostle Paul). After all, wasn't most

of the evidence merely third-party reports—essentially hearsay? I had become a typical, modern day Doubting Thomas, either yearning for more direct, personal evidence to reinforce my observations or understanding the Christian message sufficiently and fearing the obligations I would assume by accepting Christ sincerely. I liked my life and feared I might have to give up the pursuit of profile, power, and profits with which I had become so comfortable. Come to think of it, I did have something like a Damascus Road experience, or, in my case, my Afton Mountain experience. Yet, I continued to look for more. I pressed the question, "What do I know, really know?" Could I have a more immediate or personal observation that might really make a difference as to how I looked at the ultimate questions of God's existence and Christ's deity?

My internal debate itself offered an observation: self-awareness. Like some of the software installed on my new smart phone, something was always running in the background. Like Descartes, I knew that "I think." I knew that I was conscious and self-aware. What about God could I discover in that awareness?

Related to or part of this self-awareness was a recognition that humans appear to be uniquely capable of introspection, which seems to be more than mere consciousness. I knew that was true for me. I review thoughts and debate issues in my head. In a sense, I talk to myself when considering the pros and cons of taking a family vacation to the Outer Banks versus Hilton Head Island or when reviewing a client's legal problem or when considering a discourse about intelligent design. This self-awareness often became acute during long runs, particularly when I was trying to figure out how (or if) I was going to finish.

Associated with my self-awareness was a constant sense of some presence. I was talking to myself, but wasn't something or someone else also talking to me as well? Ravi Zacharias told the story of being confronted one evening after one of his lectures by an atheist who complimented him on his talk but insisted he just "wasn't buying" what Zacharias had said about Christ and faith.

Then the atheist returned the next evening and waited again to speak to Zacharias stating that he had "a few more questions." Zacharias put his arm around him and said "The Hound is on your trail." I wondered if in all of my introspection and questioning about God, the presence that I continued to feel might be the Hound of Heaven on my trail.[31]

"No One Seeks God," a sermon by Tim Keller, appeared to answer that question and confirmed what Zacharias said: God wants us and pursues us. Interestingly though, Keller indicated that we fail in our own quests for God and that without God pursuing us, we would never find him. Was this presence I felt God wrapping an arm around me just as Zacharias had put his arm around the atheist?

The sense that something or someone was talking to me was reinforced by my strong conviction that we have an active conscience. In fact, this was something else I *knew*. I have never doubted that a constant presence is guiding us in the correct direction when matters of right behavior and ethics are implicated. Our conscience helps us "do the right thing" even though we remain free to decide otherwise, something I have done often. Hence, the existence of conscience appeared tied to or bound up in our self-awareness, our capacity (if not desire) for introspection, our sense of a presence, and my affinity for the moral argument for the existence of God. Conscience requires a source, does it not?

Whenever I thought about the Trinity—Father, Son, and Holy Spirit—I always got the Holy Spirit part. In his Gospel, John wrote, "The Spirit is truth, whom the world cannot receive, because it neither sees him nor knows him, but you know him, for he dwells with you and will be in you" (John 14:17). In a very real sense, even as we laugh about skits featuring angels and devils on our shoulders, my conscience seems to be a moral agent talking to me and suggesting the proper course when a moral choice is presented. Could this presence be the Holy Spirit? With that, I began to wonder if it could be that simple.

I turned these thoughts and ideas over and over again in my mind trying to clarify and organize my observations. A close connection appeared to exist between the moral argument and conscience. Recognizing the existence of an active conscience reinforced belief in the existence of objective moral truths (after all, how could a conscience provide guidance unless a standard existed against which choices could be weighed?). In this sense recognizing the presence of an active conscience also starts one on a road that logically points to a supernatural source of objective moral truth and helps to explain the human hunger for justice.

Thus, as good lawyers often do, I reviewed, organized, and cataloged my thoughts and conclusions. I confirmed those truths of which I now thought I was sure: I knew I was self-aware; I knew of a presence; I knew I was introspective; I knew I had a conscience. I saw that the conscience appeared to be tied to a moral law—knowing what is right and wrong. It also seemed that the presence must be God's presence. If I could acknowledge his presence, did I have any choice but to acknowledge his existence?

And, if this wasn't God, what is the explanation or source for such consciousness, introspection, and moral direction? I wondered why I had not centered on this sooner. Then I recalled Ravi Zacharias saying that when the issue is recognizing and accepting God, "The biggest problem with man's unbelief is not the lack of evidence but the suppression of evidence."[32] Was that me? Despite this open and active quest, perhaps I was suppressing important evidence. Perhaps, as Keller suggested, God was pursuing me, but I was continuing to look for something else—maybe the allure of profile, profits, and power suppressed the evidence before me and continued to hinder my ability to see clearly.

In assessing whether I had been avoiding recognizing certain truths (whether I had been suppressing critical facts or conclusions), I wondered again how I knew the things that I now recognized as *true*. I didn't just fit a few premises into a logical syllogism to conclude that I had a conscience. Yet, despite that, my confidence that I knew these things was unshakeable. I had to acknowledge that we appear to know certain things without regard to rational thought or an analytical process. Certain things we understand and *know* to be true internally—seemingly by instinct or by intuition. Why or how we know by intuition was not immediately clear to me, but I was convinced that it was true.

In *Blink*,[33] author Malcolm Gladwell suggests that we know certain things independent of a traditional application of rational analysis to a set of sensory perceptions. Gladwell makes a convincing case that not only do human beings appear to have some incredible facility to analyze a situation unconsciously—something he refers to as "thin slicing" and "rapid cognition"—but that the resulting conclusions are very trustworthy. Gladwell demonstrates that our intuitive gut feelings are surprisingly reliable even though we may not know why.

With these observations from *Blink* running through my brain, I realized that one thing that I knew—really knew—was that I had a deep love for my wife and our children and that this conclusion was not the product of formal argumentation or the scientific method. I did not set down a list of sensory observations and other facts, apply a rigorous analytical method to the data, and then derive a conclusion that was compelled by the evidence. Instead, I have a commitment to my wife and daughters, and I long to be with them. I labor for their happiness without regard to any calculation of pros and cons or any evaluation of the benefits of the relationships. I know I love them without hesitation or qualification and without having to observe them or to analyze anything.

While this form of knowledge may be devoid of the analytical process, it is no less compelling. In fact, it is something I am more convinced of than many things I observe with my senses or confirm by logic and deduction. Don't we all take note of certain things we *know* to the depths of our souls? I have greater certainty of that love for them than I do of a mathematical calculation or the observation that a traffic light is red or green.

My observations about what I know intuitively—things that resonated as true in my soul—may not have been what Gladwell was talking about, but it suggested to me (consistent with what appeared to resonate from within) that we *know* certain things, though the whys and wherefores of such knowledge are less than obvious. For example, the love I have for my girls is something very real in my life. It isn't merely a description of feelings. While it may be immaterial—something I cannot touch or feel—nonetheless, it affects my physical and mental well-being. Similarly, this love is so real that it causes me to act to provide and protect—so much so that I sometimes worry about what I might be capable of doing if required to overcome a threat to those I love.

My thinking about things that I *knew* to be true but were of some other sense—not verifiable mathematically or scientifically—recalled to me some of the most profound observations by C.S. Lewis. In *Mere Christianity*, Lewis develops the moral argument by referring to something he calls the Law of Human Nature. Concerning that "law" he states:

> *Consequently, this Rule of Right and Wrong, or the Law of Human Nature, or whatever you call it, must somehow or other be a real thing—a thing that is really there, not made up by ourselves. And yet it is not a fact in the ordinary sense, in the same way as our actual behavior is a fact. It begins to look as if we shall have to admit that there is more than one kind of reality; that, in this particular case, there is something above and beyond the ordinary facts of men's behavior, and yet quite definitely real—a real law, which none of us made, but which we find pressing on us.*[34]

Just as I know that I love my family, I realized that I know other things that are real (as Lewis indicates, right from wrong), even though the source of that knowledge might not be based upon or may even conflict with traditional notions of evidence, deduction, and scientific method. Despite that lack of scientific clarity, are we any less certain?

I wondered, therefore, if knowledge of God might also be

something that I knew intuitively but had suppressed, just as I had heard Zacharias say in a number of podcasts. Perhaps I knew God existed without regard to the weight of the evidence or the length of an apologist's list of arguments. Rather, it was something I could find within if I took the time to listen. I sensed a presence in my own introspection and conscience. I had a sense of wonder and awe at the design of the natural world and the enormity of the cosmos. What more did I need?

These observations and conclusions gave me some confidence about those things that I knew intuitively. Among those things was the rightness of the Christian moral code. Christ's teachings resonated as correct. It's the way people should live. As a moral code it is brilliant, yet it is neither obvious nor intuitive. Just the opposite—it appears to conflict with our natural tendency to look out for number one. Nonetheless, upon reflection, I knew that its directives and expectations are right. The joy derived from serving others further convinced me of the rightness of Christ's moral code as that enjoyment always exceeds any benefits obtained from advancing my own cause. Traveling to Guatemala or assisting with a Habitat for Humanity house always made this clearer.

In addition, I was convinced that people should live as Christ instructed. We should all focus on a duty to serve, a desire for justice, and the need to be humble. I affirmed these beliefs as readily as I acknowledged I failed to conform to them. Perhaps most of all, recalling that I started this journey focused on those "things that endure," I had become convinced of the futility of chasing after things that do not endure. The life Christians are called to live, then, was not only another thing I knew to be correct, but a truth that endured and one I believed would endure.

Not only, therefore, did I acknowledge the correctness of the Christian moral code, but Christianity appeared to be the only worldview that made sense of life as we see and experience it— something Zacharias and others tried often to convey to stubborn listeners. Zacharias explained that a worldview coherently explains questions of origin (Where did we come from?), morality

(How do we know right from wrong?), and destiny (What happens after death?). Another of C.S. Lewis' observations came to mind. "I believe in Christianity," he said, "as I believe the sun has risen, not only because I see it, but because by it I see everything else."[35] If I interpret Lewis correctly, I believe he was saying that sensory perception ("the sun has risen") is one thing, but that being able to find a belief system that explains the world as we see and experience it ("by it I see everything else") is another thing and much more. Arguably, this was starting to look like the most powerful proof that one might find.

These various thoughts reminded me of something else I thought I *knew*. Not only did I know that the Christian message was right and the best way to live, but I also knew I wanted to be a Christian or at least I wanted to live a life like that modeled by Christ. Thus, not only did the essential truths resonate with me, but those truths appeared to have changed the lives of my friends who were Christians. I knew I wanted to be a Christian because of the way people I admired most lived: Cheryl, Carl, Bill, George, Randy, Kathy, Diane, Rob, and more. C.S. Lewis reported in his autobiography, *Surprised by Joy*, that he had a similar influence and he credited his conversion, in part, to observing his Christian friend G.K. Chesterton.

The same grace, humility, and compassion I observed in others reinforced this desire and became a persuasive force itself. I saw it in an old college friend and her husband who had committed to bringing education, health care, and the Christian message to an extraordinarily dangerous part of the Middle East. It was there in my new friends in Guatemala and my fellow missionaries to that country who exhibited a quiet confidence in their faith and a desire to act upon those beliefs. It was a law partner who discounted his contributions, declined compensation increases, and demonstrated every day how much can be accomplished when no one insists on taking the credit.

These were not the dim-witted folks Richard Dawkins made all Christians out to be, nor were they bitter people "clinging to guns and religion." I recalled Zacharias saying that the world has five Gospels: Matthew, Mark, Luke, John, and the Christian, and that most people only read that last one. In other words, the way Christians live speaks most loudly. And from those in my life, accepting Christ apparently made them into people I wanted to emulate. They were running the race in the way I wanted to run the race.

Interestingly, I noted that these observations were consistent with many in the Roman world during the early centuries after Christ's death. Many credit the rise and spread of Christianity not to intellectual appeal, but to the unselfish compassion and generosity of Christ's followers. Historians record that people in the ancient world were surprised, impressed, and incredulous at how Christians lived and treated others. While I don't have space here to develop the evidence, among the items I studied included how Emperor Julian insisted that his priests match the virtue of the early Christians ("Galileans"), who not only started hospitals and orphanages but also nursed the sick during plagues at great risk to themselves. Julian wrote, "The impious Galileans support not only their poor but ours as well, everyone can see our people lack aid from us."[36]

As I developed these observations about the rightness of the Christian message and about that which we appear to know intuitively, I recalled reading an argument for God's existence, attributed to C.S. Lewis, known as the argument from desire. Lewis observed that human beings do not have any innate, natural desires for which a real object does not exist that can satisfy the desire. (If man was hungry, food existed to satisfy that desire.) Thus, as Lewis observed, because man has a desire for God, an "object" to satisfy that desire must exist, which, of course, is God.

I continued to work through these thoughts and doubts. Things seemed to make sense more and more. Coherence was coming into view. Christianity seemed like the best explanation for everything I was thinking and observing. Collecting my thoughts, I again took a mental inventory of everything I *knew*. I knew I had an active conscience. I knew the world had right and wrong. I knew Jesus Christ was not a myth but a real person in history. I knew the resurrection had to be true. I knew the Christian message was correct. I knew I wanted to be a Christian. Perhaps I didn't need to rely on third-party reports, observations from the natural world, or logical syllogisms. I seemed to have gained a confidence that the Doubting Thomas within me sought.

Although I thought I was ready, I did not act upon the conclusions I was starting to draw. The evidence and arguments were clearly compelling—certainly the most compelling of the alternative explanations. I needed to bite the bullet and acknowledge that this all made sense so that I could go back and recite the Apostles' Creed and live an honest life of faith without hesitation or doubt. But for some reason, I still delayed. I deferred making any decision or commitment. I looked for more books, listened to more podcasts, and wondered if I needed to analyze the arguments more intently and to review these matters further. What else might help tip the scales one way or the other, once and for all?

I found one. I had been trained to recognize that despite how compelling an argument might be, another side to the story always exists. Just as I would do as an attorney, therefore, I decided I should look at these same arguments from the perspective of an adversary.

CHAPTER 15

PARTICIPATING IN A MAJOR

... let us run with perseverance the race that is set before us.

—Hebrews 12:1 (NRSV)

Although I had been running for a couple of years, most people who knew me still thought of me as a golfer, not as a runner. In fact, most knew that I am as passionate about golf history and architecture as I am about playing the game. I write a regular column on golf course architecture, and I rate courses for *Golfweek*'s "Top 100" courses. I've written three regional golf histories, including the history of the Arnold Palmer's Bay Hill Club in Orlando, Florida, and I serve as an officer and board member for the Virginia State Golf Association.

Considering my level of interest in golf, no one would be surprised that arriving for a noon tee time was almost as religious as attendance at Christ Lutheran immediately before this regularly scheduled round. I was part of a fairly regular foursome, which included John who also attended Christ Lutheran. Because not everyone made every week, we tried to give each other a heads up if we could not play the next week. Hence, one Sunday in April, as we walked from the fifth green to the sixth tee, I mentioned that I would not be playing the following week because I would be out of town. Immediately recalling that I was scheduled to run in the

Boston Marathon, our friend Giff said, without missing a beat, that now he'd have two friends that participated in a "major." I had never thought of it that way. Unlike Giff's other friend, I was never going to play Baltusrol *during* the US Open or Augusta National *during* The Masters, but he was correct that I was going to run from Hopkinton to Boston in the same race on the same day as the very best distance runners in the world.

A week later, and almost a year after I ran in Scotland, my biggest running weekend had arrived. I tried to keep a modest exterior, but, in fact, I was nearly giddy with excitement. I was going to run in the Boston Marathon, the pinnacle event in distance running.

The Boston Marathon is the oldest annual marathon in United States. Its roots go back to 1896 when the modern Olympics began. In resurrecting the ancient athletic competitions, the international sports world staged a marathon run based on the story of Pheidippides. A year later, John Graham, a team manager for the U.S. at the inaugural Olympics and a member of the Boston Athletic Association, organized a marathon footrace in America. On April 19, 1897, fifteen runners competed on a 24.5 mile route from Metcalf's Mill in Ashland, Massachusetts, to downtown Boston. The start was moved to Hopkinton in 1924, and in 1927, the official distance of the Boston Marathon increased to 26.2 miles.

I had an early morning flight to Boston a few days before the race. I checked in and made my way to the gate, where I noticed ten or twelve runners, some with familiar faces, also waiting for Jet Blue to take us to Beantown. Ambivalence set in almost immediately. What business do I have participating in this sacred—at least for runners—event?

If a badge of honor in long distance running circles exists, it's qualifying to run in the Boston Marathon. The standards are rigorous. Men under thirty have to complete a qualifying marathon in at least three hours and ten minutes. For someone my age, the qualifying time is three hours and thirty-five minutes. The best that I had done was 4:57:28—nearly an hour and a half off the pace.

On the other hand, I wasn't a "bandit," runners who join the race even though they are not registered. I was registered and had an official entry, but I would be running in the back of the pack with the other "charity runners." But I wasn't exactly a charity runner either. My law partner in Boston had helped me gain entry even though I lacked a qualifying time. Nonetheless, wondering if I should really be heading for Boston, I was beginning to burst my own bubble.

We landed on time, and I met one of my law partners from Norfolk who had actually qualified. After taking a cab to our hotel, we headed across the Boston Common and found our way to Boylston Street, the finish line, and the convention hall where we could pick up our bibs and visit the expo. Anxiety grew as I hung out with people who, in my mind, were the *real* runners. Checking into our hotel the desk clerk congratulated me on qualifying for the race. As I left the elevator before heading over to registration another runner (a real runner) wished me good luck for the race. I began to feel dirty, as though I were soiling this cherished tradition by sneaking in the back door. I felt as though I were crashing the party.

Perhaps the ultimate expression of this uncleanness was when I stopped to pick up my bright yellow, official Boston Marathon training shirt. One of the volunteers asked how many I had run. Without thinking about what he was asking, I said five, which led him to ask if I had run through the heat in the 2001 Boston Marathon. Distress and panic set in immediately. I now understood. He meant, how many times had I run in the *Boston* Marathon. You see, Boston is not just another marathon; it's Boston! You don't need to say "the Boston Marathon." Committed runners know that it's just "Boston."

I decided in a split second that the shirt I was trying would be fine and that I needed to get out of there before I was exposed as the cheat I felt I was. My naïve visit to the Boston expos reminded me of the old advice that it's better to keep your mouth shut and let all the world think you a fool then to open your mouth and remove all doubt. And for any real runners that might read this, here is my solemn pledge: I will not run in Boston again unless I qualify.

After getting settled in the hotel and completing the race registration, my law partner Ray and I split up to visit different friends. My afternoon and evening were spent visiting a college roommate I hadn't seen for twenty years. While I had gained some weight and my hair was gray, Ron looked like he did in 1977-78 when we shared a dorm room in Williamsburg. In fact, I roomed with Ron when I ran that first marathon in Virginia Beach. I must have been at his home for fifteen or twenty minutes before he realized I was actually running in the marathon. He thought my firm or a firm client was doing something in connection with the race and I was there for that reason.

Seeing Ron and his wife Karen was great. They and their two boys are good athletes. Ron had been on the William & Mary gymnastic team, and we had played a number of intramural sports together, including soccer. He still played soccer pretty competitively. We caught up some more over dinner at a local Argentinean steakhouse, but by 11:00, I had to head back to my hotel. I would have avoided the wine and the red meat if it had been the night before the race, but with another day to go I thought I'd survive.

The next morning I headed out for a light jog. My hotel was just a block down the hill from the State House, so I had the benefit of running through the Boston Common and the Public Garden. With some of my guilt in check, I ran through the Common among many others who were obviously loosening up for the next day as well. It was exhilarating, and I found some of my apprehension about belonging beginning to fade.

Later that morning, I walked over to the finish line, where runners, family members and others were already congregating, snapping photographs and dreaming of good finishes. I met up with Ray, and we found a subway to Fenway Park to enjoy a pleasant afternoon at an iconic stadium where the home team won. Then we were off to one of the many Italian restaurants in the North End for the obligatory, pre-race pasta dinner.

Similar to New York, Boston is a big marathon with about 25,000 runners. (New York has over 40,000!) Like New York, Boston is a point-to-point race as opposed to Richmond, Edinburgh and Charlottesville, which are circuit races, finishing at or near the start point. And like New York, because of its size and the point-to-point nature of the race, Boston has significant logistical problems.

On race morning, Ray and I waited in line at the edge of the Boston Common, down the hill from the State House, to catch one of the chartered buses that would take us to the race's start. As with New York, the bus ride seemed to take a very long time, but eventually we drove into Hopkinton, circled the local high school, and emptied out into the school grounds for a three-hour wait.

New York also had a long wait before the race began. I sat, rested, and fought off nervous energy. Along with all the other runners, I alternated between hydrating and emptying my bladder, and I munched on my official pre-race breakfast of a bagel with peanut butter and a banana. I was really getting ready to run in the Boston Marathon!

Eventually the call came for the various waves, beginning with the fastest. Ray, having qualified for the race, headed off for the start line long before I did. I spoke to some other charity runners and was able to share a few experiences and thoughts about such a long race. For many, this was to be their first 26.2-mile run. Our call finally came and we began the walk from the staging area to the start line in downtown Hopkinton, shedding unnecessary clothes and leaving them in bags for Goodwill.

I got into the proper starting corral, near the very end of the runners. Gathering a few yards farther back were the bandits, mostly college-age runners without bibs. This, I learned, was a tradition, and race officials really didn't police the corral lines at this point. As in most mega-runs, we walked to the start line and as we crossed, the timing chip attached to our shoes signaled to the computer that we had begun the trek east toward downtown Boston.

The beginning of the racecourse has a completely different feel to it from New York's. This route is a county road heading east out of Hopkinton that bends and rolls as it cuts through the New England countryside. While every inch of the NYC route is packed with spectators, the early miles of the Boston route is only punctuated here and there with clusters of people sitting at country restaurants, homes, and businesses. Too much vegetation lines the road for race fans to line both sides. Three and a half miles after leaving Hopkinton, we reached Ashland, with its large clock tower. This was the original start for the marathon until it moved to Hopkinton in 1924.

Boston is run on Patriot's Day, a public holiday unique to Massachusetts. Most of the locals had the day off from work, and many had gathered for pre-race breakfasts, other refreshments, and race watching. While the spectators may have been spread out in the early miles of the race, they were no less vocal than the fans in New York. Their encouragement and support is truly remarkable; keep in mind that, by the time my pack of runners came by, they had already been watching and cheering for a couple of hours.

The road toward Mile 4 was gradually downhill, and I felt swept along by my fellow runners as well as the topography. I thoroughly enjoyed those early miles, the ease with which they seemed to flow by, and the intimacy of the route. Around Mile 6 we came into Framingham and ran by the railroad station where, in 1907, a train interfered with the race. Only the six lead runners got through the area before the train blocked the route. At this point the crowds appeared to be thinner. They didn't have the mass and depth of the crowds through much of Brooklyn; officials estimate 500,000 fans in Boston compared with two million in New York. Before we reached the halfway point, the route took us through the beautiful town of Natick where eager, encouraging race fans again lined the route.

Despite reputation, one thing that usually surprises first-time Boston Marathon runners are the "girls of Wellesley College." I was surprised. Hours into the race, the co-eds still came out for the slower runners and still maintained their volume of cheering. The scene was pretty crazy with the "Free Kisses" and the "Kiss Me" signs and banners. And almost unlimited actual kisses were available for the willing. As a father of similarly-aged girls, I passed on the kisses, but took lots of high fives and plenty of energy from their enthusiasm. The terrain rolled through the college and shortly after the "Screech Tunnel," we passed the midpoint in downtown Wellesley.

In a word, the fans were fantastic. Many offered unofficial water stops, oranges, pretzels, gummy bears, and other food items. And, like New York, my favorite unofficial support center was a woman offering baby wipes. The chance to have a cool wipe to remove some of the sweat and grit from my face was most welcome.

Boston is known for its hills as the route approaches Newton. These hills would not be particularly difficult if they didn't come when they do—between Mile 18 and Mile 21, when runners are hitting the wall as their stores of glycogen are running out. Thus, the hills come at the precise time that many runners first begin to struggle.

The route dips to about sixty feet above sea level and then returns to two hundred thirty feet as runners climb the Newton Hills. Unlike the current fad of trying to offer runners the fastest marathon route, Boston demands that runners conquer a series of four hills (though some say seven). These culminate with the largest one, Heartbreak Hill. I became somewhat discouraged a little after Mile 16 as I ran down a long hill knowing I'd have to make up that elevation *and* deal with the hills that would follow.

My objective was to finish the Boston Marathon in five hours, but long before I started the race, I had added this goal: I would *not* walk up Heartbreak Hill. I knew my stamina, and I knew that

I would probably hit the wall between eighteen and twenty miles, but I also remembered what my caddie at Cypress Point told me as we arrived at the tee of the famous 16th Hole. As we looked across the crashing ocean between us and the green, two hundred forty yards away, he announced what I already knew, "No one is going to ask you what you shot, but they will ask you what you did on the 16th Hole." After running Boston, few would ask my time, but they would want to know how I did on Heartbreak Hill. I wanted to have an answer similar to the one I have for that day on the world's most famous par three.

So I mentally prepared myself and "ran" up Heartbreak Hill. It is a real hill that goes on for .37 miles to be precise. Keeping up any pace was very difficult, but I wanted to meet my goal. I pressed on, going slowly but steadily all the way to the top. I was so fatigued by the time I got to the top I barely noticed the cheering Boston College students lining the crest. Once I conquered Heartbreak Hill, I rested with four or five minutes of walking. "Now, let's finish," I thought to myself as I picked up my pace and started running again.

After Heartbreak Hill, the rest of the race really is downhill. I glanced at my GPS watch. I was still near the pace I needed to break five hours, but I was out of gas. Like the other marathons I had run, the last five miles were just plain hard—and no fun at all. Each time I had completed a long race, I said "Never again," but within a day, the experience and thoughts of a renewed challenge convinced me to give it another try. I was at the "never-again" point *again*. Nothing hurt; I was just dead. But I had to figure out a way to get to the finish. I shuffled along, mixing running with some walking breaks. My back began to ache, and I wanted to sit down. I was tempted to just quit; but this was the Boston Marathon, and I was going to get to the finish somehow.

I later determined that if I was spending five hours on my feet, I was forcing my torso to support a lot of weight for a long time. No wonder it was tired and achy. One of the fixes for this problem (other than, as many people urged, "Stop running so far!") is core training, something that our MTT coaches and our training book advised and I ignored. Studies show fairly persuasively that by strengthening core muscles, runners are able to maintain better form, remain better stabilized, improve balance and efficiency, and reduce the risk of injury. My back was telling me that next time I'd better work on developing my core before attempting another marathon.

Sadly I have no memory of running through Brookline. I say "sadly" not because I missed the hometown of one of golf's finest courses and the site of one of golf's most historic moments—when in 1913 local caddie Francis Ouimet defeated the best from Britain in "the greatest game ever played"—but because my "running" was pathetic. I was spent and still had to figure out a way to get back to Boylston Street, four miles away. As I descended from BC, I hit a low point emotionally as well. For the first time, I started to feel very alone. Finally, I had reached the outskirts of the city. As I stumbled along, I saw signs of urban life. Gone are the green spaces and country roads of Newton, replaced by high-density housing and divided four-lane roadways. What didn't change was the presence and enthusiasm of the Boston crowds. By now the route followed Beacon Street as the runners continue east, slightly downhill toward the John Hancock Building and the finish line.

One of my law partners who had run Boston the prior year told me to look for the CITGO billboard as I came into Boston proper. "You'll know you're almost finished when you see that sign," he said. Finally, I reached the CITGO sign and passed by Fenway Park on my right. Only a mile to go.

I knew then that, one way or another, I was going to finish. My GPS watch indicated that it was still possible to break five hours. If I could run the last mile in about thirteen minutes, I could do it. If I had not just run twenty-five miles, running a thirteen-minute mile would have been easy. I was shot, but I was going to finish; so I concentrated on picking my feet up and putting them down just a little longer. After half a mile, I could see Boylston Street and the left-hand turn onto the final stretch. As I made the turn I could see good crowds still lining both sides of Boylston Street.

To my disappointment, the finish was much farther down the street than I was expecting. It seemed as though I had least a half-mile still to go. Actually it was much closer to a quarter-mile, but I was worried for a second considering how few moments I still had to complete the course in less than five hours.

Somehow, I picked up the pace, and as I did, the cheering seemed to swell perhaps because it appeared that I was moving quickly as I passed many runners who were walking to the finish. I looked at my watch again. It would be close, but I thought I could do it as long as nothing cramped up. I looked straight ahead toward the blue and gold John Hancock/Boston Marathon banners and the finish line. I kept my legs moving, crossed the finish line, and pressed the stop key. 4:59:13! I had done it with 47 seconds to spare.

Volunteers placed a medal around my neck and wrapped me in a space blanket. I was a little unstable physically and accepted the volunteer's assistance as I hobbled to the rest area. I was getting cold and had a little trouble walking, but I kept shuffling down Boylston Street toward my hotel just beyond the Boston Common. I recalled the walk back to Times Square in New York and how much it had helped my recovery; so with my goodie bag of a bagel, energy drink, and a few other things in hand, I walked on.

I headed through the Public Garden, across the Swan Boat Lagoon Bridge, up the Boston Common, below the State House, and another block to my hotel. I had finished the Boston Marathon. The race may have taken me more than twice as long as the elite runners and longer than ninety percent of the field, but on this one day I had participated in one of the world's greatest sporting events.

CHAPTER 16

ARE WE KIDDING OURSELVES? THE GOD DELUSION

*Numbers don't lie. You always seem to remember your workouts
as being a little better than they were.
It's good to go back and review what you do.*

—Frank Shorter

In the movie version of *Angels & Demons*, the prequel to *The Da-Vinci Code*, Tom Hanks's character responds to a question about belief in God by saying, "Faith is a gift I have yet to receive." My regular golfing partner John had used this quote during a sermon he had given on lay Sunday, explaining that he never remembered a time when he didn't believe. When my friend, Carl, read the earliest drafts of this manuscript, he said the same thing. Wow! I thought. Why wasn't it that easy for me?

Perhaps it is a hazard of my legal training or part of my nature, but I delight in challenging assumptions, debating points, questioning authority, and arguing the opposite side of propositions. Sadly, Cheryl can readily confirm this character flaw. Even when the point at issue mattered little, I enjoyed playing the devil's advocate. More than anything, though, I believe it was this training, or my nature, or more likely a combination of the two feeding on each other that forced me on in this journey of faith. In many respects, I really don't think I had a choice.

Jesus said we will never enter the kingdom of God unless we become like children (Mark 10:15). I don't know what theologians and other commentators say this means, but to me it suggests that we need to strip away our doubts, jettison our devil's advocacy, and accept God with a childlike innocence unaffected by sophisticated and nuanced arguments about existence, or intelligent design, or other issues.

That said, I think that among the barriers before me was my intellectual arrogance, my conviction that I could figure out most things if I just put my mind to it. This self-reliance and self-confidence were among my most dominant attributes. Another barrier, I believe, was my legal training and the ability to spin things almost any way possible to advance my clients' objectives. I could do that until we both started believing our own story regardless of accuracy or the soundness of our position.

Foundational to the practice of law is the adversary process. In theory, the point-counterpoint of that process should reveal the truth. I probably believe that as a general matter. On the other hand, I have found that the process of zealous advocacy sometimes causes us attorneys to start accepting the creative reasoning and faulty logic we impose on a set of facts to help a client's cause. Right or wrong, I operate very comfortably on this plane. I relish the opportunity to respond to an adversary's memorandum of law, to demonstrate why my client's position is more sound, and to argue that my adversary's arguments border on the frivolous if not the ridiculous.

In the practice of law, no one knows the problems or holes in a legal position better than the advocate himself. As lawyers, if we are honest with ourselves and if we are preparing as best we can, we must seriously consider the arguments of our opposing counsel. To be too convinced of our own cause and the brilliance of the advocacy is an almost certain step toward disaster. I needed to confront directly the arguments made by atheists against the ideas that had become so attractive and convincing to me. How persuasive were their explanations? Could I accept or refute their arguments?

One of the most prominent of the so-called new atheists is Richard Dawkins who wrote *The God Delusion*,[37] perhaps the most thorough, recent articulation of the atheists' contention that any belief in God is irrational. Could my renewed disposition to recommit to Christianity survive the open attack by an eminent scientist and Oxford University scholar? I thought examining *The God Delusion* was the kind of a challenge I had to face, a gauntlet I had to run if I were ever going to complete my journey. The need for this confrontation became particularly acute when I read Dawkins's stated objective in his Preface: "If this book works as I intend, religious leaders who open it would be atheists when they put it down."[38]

For my purposes here, recognizing that a thorough treatment is beyond the scope of a single chapter, I focus on his response to what I've called the moral argument for the existence of God, the idea that the existence of human morality is a basis for the belief in God. I did this because I found the moral argument the most compelling. I wondered whether Dawkins could offer a satisfactory explanation for our sense of right and wrong without God and a naturalistic explanation for why so many people act altruistically. As it turned out, Dawkins devoted an entire chapter to these questions, asking, "Why Are We Good?"

In responding to the moral argument, Dawkins attempts to show that any moral sense and any human goodness are the result of natural selection. Initially, he acknowledges that Darwinism more readily explains "hunger, fear and sexual lust" than empathy, decency, and pity. Similarly, he acknowledges, "Mercy to a debtor is, when seen out of context, as un-Darwinian as adopting someone else's child."[39] So Dawkins asks, "Where does the Good Samaritan in us come from?" I was excited to read this. Dawkins was posing and presumably preparing to answer the very questions I wanted to ask him.

In crafting a reply, Dawkins posited, "Genes ensure their selfish survival by influencing organisms to behave altruistically."[40] He then goes on to say that two "fairly well understood" circumstances exist where natural selection chooses the selfless. He refers to these as "the two pillars of altruism in the Darwinian world."[41] The first pillar is encouraging the continuation of "genetic kin." This pillar, apparently introduced by Darwin in his *Origin of Species*, attempts to explain why an organism might favor another at cost to itself, to its own survival. The second pillar he calls "reciprocal altruism," the basis of trade and barter among humans.[42]

Dawkins devotes only half a paragraph to explaining the supposed "first pillar"—"genetic kin"—and never raises it again. Regarding "reciprocal altruism," Dawkins suggests that, in human beings, the fostering of a reputation for altruism is another explanation for moral behavior. But didn't Dawkins miss the point? Isn't running around doing altruistic things in order to bolster your reputation rather than in order to do the right thing what most of us call hypocrisy? In this, I thought Dawkins was attempting to lift "reciprocal altruism" by its own bootstraps.

As I analyzed the underlying concept of reciprocal altruism, I concluded that what he explained wasn't altruism at all. Instead Dawkins had subtly changed the subject. He had deflected a discussion of why people do good without the expectation of something in return, which is altruism, to a discussion of behavior that's motivated by an expectation of benefit, that is, something that "reciprocates." *Webster's Dictionary* defines altruism as the "unselfish regard for or devotion to the welfare of others."[43] Similarly, the *Encyclopedia Britannica* states that, in the field of ethics, altruism is "a theory of conduct that regards the good of others as the end of moral action."[44] Evidently the objective or end of Dawkins's "reciprocal altruism" is to gain an advantage for oneself, not to do good for someone else.

As a lawyer, of course, I like to think that I am prepared for this type of challenge in the process of developing and participating in argumentation. Here Dawkins was using a common, but clever, rhetorical device. If you can't effectively refute a proposition, or if you don't have a clear reply, change the question or alter a premise—but do so with careful subtlety hoping no one notices. If the reader doesn't perceive the shift, he or she may adopt the conclusions that follow once the question is altered.

Dawkins presses this device by concluding simply, but seemingly with authority, that this type of altruism has a "well worked out Darwinian rationale." But he never elaborates on what that rationale is, concluding that something is just so without explaining it is also a logical fallacy. Dawkins simply begs the question.

This failure is particularly troublesome. He acknowledges that human instinct resulting from natural selection leads us, in the first instance, to selfish behavior. Thus, the burden of proof faced by Dawkins concerning altruism is particularly high because he has acknowledged that the existence of altruism is an exception to the general rule of evolution, the bedrock principle from which all of his analysis flows.

Dawkins spends nearly five hundred pages explaining, reiterating, and justifying his position in his recent book, *The Greatest Show on Earth*.[45] In the language of my profession, we might expect "clear and convincing evidence," but none is forthcoming. Instead, Dawkins summarily attempts to explain away an exception to his rule by saying that "well worked out Darwinian rationale" nonetheless applies. No one would ever get away with that in court.

Ultimately, Dawkins is not up to the task. Because "reciprocal altruism" is not altruism at all, Dawkins doesn't answer the very question he poses: "Where does the Good Samaritan in us come from?" I wondered how and why he missed this, since in his own rejection of Pascal's Wager (elsewhere in *The God Delusion*), he recognized that sincerity is a necessary component of any real belief. If someone is altruistic because he expects some later benefit to be returned, he lacks all sincerity and an "unselfish regard for others." Dawkins may have found a couple of organisms under his microscope that are interested in reciprocal altruism, but he has done nothing to answer the very real, very human question of why we help others where no gain or benefit is anticipated.

Reciprocal altruism, then, is not an adequate explanation. What about "genetic kin"—the tendency to favor our own? I can't see how or why this explains altruism. In fact, in a very curious touch of irony, the Good Samaritan was not only altruistic with no expectation of gain, recognition, or reciprocation, but he provided for a Jew, a member of group that despised Samaritans and that Samaritans despised. The beaten Jewish traveler was not in any way his genetic kin. Recall that two Jews who were genetic kin, a Levite and a priest, had passed by the injured traveler to avoid any contact at all, behavior that would appear inconsistent with Darwinism and an instinct for self-preservation.

Maybe I was missing something. Maybe this all works out as Dawkins describes it in his laboratories. I just don't see how it plays out in any manner at all in the real world of personal conduct and human interaction. Stated differently, Dawkins's explanations are, in addition to being intellectually inadequate, particularly unsatisfying because they bear no relation to or connection with human experience.

I had expected that Dawkins might try to use human guilt to explain altruistic behavior, but I was wrong. He never suggests guilt as a basis for altruistic conduct, and he never explains why it can't be a source. I decided that the absence was probably intentional, then I recalled a variety of podcasts concerning the moral argument and ethics. In one particular message R. C. Sproul argues that the most likely source of guilt is our own recognition of either our failure to do that which we know we should do or our failure to refrain from doing that which we know we should not do. In other words, Sproul would suggest that the source of guilt is our refusal to accept and act upon our moral obligations. If this is the case, then for Dawkins, a discussion of guilt would go somewhere he does not want to go because he would then need to explain the source for any such moral obligations.

Near the end of his discussion of these issues of morality and ethical behavior, even Dawkins appears to acknowledge that his explanation is not intellectually satisfying. He recognizes this when he attempts to explain random acts of kindness in a modern, urban society where few circumstances such as kinship are present. This leads him to make two remarkable statements that border on surrender. First, he admits, seemingly for convenience, that natural selection does not have unlimited reach in explaining human conduct. Second, he wonders if true altruism is in fact just "misfirings" or "Darwinian mistakes."[46] This is conduct that doesn't comport with the rule of natural selection that advances one organism over another.

This explanation complete with "misfirings" appears to be more honest intellectually, but it naturally requires one to ask what has become of the "pillars" of the Darwinian explanations for kindness and generosity. In truth, Dawkins has no answer to the question, "Why are we good?" other than his assertion that such behavior is an aberration, a Darwinian mistake.

Perhaps Dawkins recognized the paucity of his arguments for human goodness and decided that a clever rather than a direct approach of the issues would serve his purposes. An end run is often a good approach when a frontal assault fails.

I say this because Dawkins begins his chapter on morality by quoting passages from hate mail received by other atheists. (Dawkins apparently could not rely on his own mail to find something extreme enough to adequately distract the reader.) The passages are filled with emotional, anti-intellectual, and dreadful *ad hominem* attacks: "Satan worshipping scum .... Please die and go to hell. . . . I hope you get a painful disease like rectal cancer and die a slow painful death . . ."[47] But, I wondered what Dawkins's point was in repeating this stuff. If he intended to undertake a rational discourse of a serious subject, why select a few irrational letters from extremists, who may be theists or Christians? Was Dawkins really suggesting that these letters exhibit mainstream approach to these questions taken by people like Keller or Zacharias? Again this sadly appears to show an amateurish reliance distracting the reader from rational analysis to an emotional appeal—another logical fallacy.

One form of clever lawyering is for an attorney with a weak response to the issue before the court to try to change the issue by suggesting that he or she is "just" rephrasing it. That is, if you don't like the question before the court because it leads to an answer that's not in your favor, try to change the question. If you succeed, you have a question that results in conclusions you want.

Dawkins is a master at this ruse. In *The God Delusion,* he favorably cites fellow atheist Michael Shermer who, in his book *The Science of Good and Evil* sets up the following apparent syllogism:

> *If you agree that, in the absence of God, that you would "commit robbery, rape and murder," you reveal yourself as a immoral person.... If on the other hand, you admit that you would continue to be a good person even if not under divine surveillance, you have fatally undermined your claim that God is necessary for us to be good.*[48]

That sounds compelling, but its logic wouldn't survive in a freshman philosophy course.

If you assume away the most fundamental precept in an argument, you can usually reach any conclusion you want. Shermer's choice has some appeal if you accept his premises, but no one would do that. We don't refrain from rape and murder because we believe in God. Christians recognize that the source of this moral code is God, but it does not follow that they refrain from criminal acts because they believe in God. We refrain from rape and murder because we *know* it's wrong. I never reasoned from God or the absence of God. I recognized first a sense of right and wrong. I then reasoned back to a source of that morality. No theist says, "I believe in God so I have determined that I should not steal."

If Dawkins's opening alone wasn't enough to raise questions about his analytical method, the closing arguments to his chapter on morality confirm his uneven, thrashing, and illogical approach to important questions.

Using information from Steven Pinker's *The Blank Slate*, Dawkins ties his conclusions about human altruism to the riots in Montreal during a 1969 police strike.[49] He begins by asking, "Wasn't the Montreal strike a pretty good natural experiment to test the hypothesis that belief in God makes us good?"[50] Then without any evidence or reasoning, he states that "presumably" a majority of people in Montreal believed in God. Given that unsubstantiated presumption, he then wonders why their belief did not cause the people to restrain themselves, concluding that a belief in God has no affect on morality. Upon analysis, the inclusion of this haphazard material backfires badly.

I can only imagine the questioning and criticism I'd receive from a judge if I made that kind of argument in court. I can hear it now, "So, Mr. Matson, even assuming your presumption is correct, how many people were in Montreal? Were most of those people witnessed robbing and destroying? Were over a million criminal acts committed? Is it possible that some of those three million did not rob and riot? And why do we assume that most of the rioters believed in God? In fact, given the 'presumption' within your argument that most people in Montreal believed in God and only a fraction of those people participated in the rioting, isn't it just as likely, or *even more likely*, that the people involved in the criminal conduct were that small portion of the Montreal population who did *not* believe in God?"

Dawkins continues to pad the chapter and add to this line of fallacious reasoning when he adopts material from fellow atheist Sam Harris. In a *Letter to a Christian Nation*, Harris attempts to undermine any correlation between religious belief and "societal health" by attempting to show that more crime occurs in Republican dominated red states than in Democratic dominated blue states.[51] He does this by focusing on the murder and burglary rates of the cities in those states. To begin with, he makes an unsupported assumption that the "overwhelming influence of conservative Christians" causes a state to be red. This is ridiculous. First, whether a state is "red" or "blue" might easily be determined by a vote of 54–46, 52–48 or even 50.5–49.5. Their generalizations don't make much sense if the margins are small.

More significantly, Dawkins freely adopts Harris' methodology. Harris states, and Dawkins repeats, "of the 25 most dangerous cities, 76 percent are in red states and 24 percent are in blue states."[52] This, however, ignores the fact that most cities including the cities in red states are blue. For example, Pennsylvania is a red State, but Pittsburgh and Philadelphia are reliably blue. Yet Harris and Dawkins don't trouble themselves with whether those "dangerous cities" are red or blue. That would appear to be more relevant assuming their correlation study has any usefulness or credibility. Recall again that the underlying assumption, supported nowhere by any evidence, is that conservative Christians cause a state to be red.

We can understand and forgive someone making one of these mistakes. But Dawkins draws conclusions from data without recognizing that a number of steps in logic are missing. These are certainly not "proofs."

Dawkins is an educated and sophisticated scholar, so we can reasonably assume he knows exactly what he is doing. Nonetheless, he persisted in his "arguments," believing that his audience is either uneducated or unsophisticated, or even more likely, that they are so predisposed to his conclusions that they will accept them with abandon.

Dawkins seemingly cannot help himself. Just when I thought the discussion had reached the level of absurdity, Dawkins suggests with no studies or arguments that prisons hold few atheists: "Atheists are smarter than theists and they eschew criminal behavior, which I guess means that Christians or theists are more inclined to criminal and, therefore, immoral conduct."[53] Really?! Then almost out of nowhere, contributing to the disorganization of the chapter, he postulates, "Another good possibility is that atheism is correlated with some third factor, such as higher education, intelligence or reflectiveness."[54] Dawkins appears to believe sincerely that the more educated and more intelligent individuals—a group that Dawkins obviously believes includes him—don't believe in God because the irrationality of that position is obvious to them.

I had to conclude that Dawkins didn't write the book for someone on an honest quest. Rather, he apparently wrote the book to make money and pander to individuals already inclined to agree with him.

One could dismiss my analysis even more quickly than I dismissed Dawkins's by concluding that I have a bias or an agenda. Yet, of that person I would ask, what function did inflammatory letters play in the substance of honest debate? Why utilize logically deficient arguments? Why not engage substantively and meaningfully with the thoughtful presentations of these issues by people like Zacharias, Keller, Colson, and Sproul? Why not answer the question you said you were going to address?

Time and space (and proper balance) do not permit a full examination of *The God Delusion* here. As a general matter, however, Dawkins insists that a rational or "scientific" study of the question of God can lead only to one conclusion: anyone who accepts that a transcendent God exists suffers from a delusion—a false belief held in the face of strong contradictory evidence. I had been hoping to understand Dawkins's "strong contradictory evidence," but was unimpressed and certainly not convinced.

Let me add that we catch a glimpse of not only his purpose, but also his personality when he borrows this line from a novel: "When one person suffers from a delusion, it is called insanity. When many people suffer from a delusion it is called Religion."[55] Dawkins is condescending at best and hateful at worse. As an attorney, I learned that belittling your opponent, mocking his or her arguments, and lacing your own argument with biting sarcasm do nothing to help your case. Good judges assume that the question under consideration is worthy of a fair, impartial decision and that the positions of the opposing parties are worthy of a fair hearing. Readers of *The God Delusion* should be just as dispassionate as a good judge, trying to discern arguments pro and con and coming to a fair conclusion. I was surprised and disappointed that Dawkins laced his opening with such venom and his arguments with such faulty logic and bias. If I were to borrow a line from someone else's book, I'd borrow from *The Brothers Karamazov* where Dostoyevsky writes, "If there is no God, everything is permitted." Dawkins's world has no immutable standard of right and wrong—and if I knew one thing, I knew that certain things are unquestionably right or wrong.

Somewhere in the process of trying to appreciate the contrary arguments, I realized I had made my decision about what I believed. In part, I had to acknowledge that although I undertook a serious, essentially legal analysis of the questions presented by Dawkins's book, my bias—my inclination to accept Christianity as true—welled up to the top as I worked through the chapter.

Despite having arrived at that new or renewed point of reference, I still hadn't internalized or acted upon my conclusions. Why? I started to wonder if I really had more questions and needed additional support for the conclusions I was drawing, if I was just enjoying an intellectual exercise, or if something else was happening. In particular, I wondered if I had continued my journey and deferred any real decisions not because I didn't know the answer, but because I was scared of the consequences of the conclusions I had already reached. Perhaps I didn't want to face the reality of what it all meant and feared that accepting Christ might require some uncomfortable changes. Christianity might impose obligations and expectations on me that I wasn't ready to accept. I still liked my life and was comfortable relying on my own efforts to achieve whatever it was that I sought. But, how much longer was I going to drag this out?

CHAPTER 17

WINNING THE RACE

You can't lose this race because you're not running against anyone else. You're only running against yourself, and as long as you are running, you are winning.

—Amby Burfoot

I have fought the good fight, I have finished the race, I have kept the faith.

—2 Timothy 4:7 (NIV)

During my journey of investigating my faith and learning to run, I spent a year participating in a leadership program in Richmond, known as Leadership Metro Richmond or LMR. After our graduation reception, I found myself in an impromptu discussion with several of my LMR classmates during which the question of spirituality, religion, and inevitably, Christianity came up. Our class leader, Bob, mentioned that he had grown up in the Lutheran Church (coincidentally at Christ Lutheran) and had gone to parochial school but couldn't accept the church anymore. Bob explained that he believed Jesus was a great man and a great role model, but he didn't accept him as God or Lord. Bob insisted he was very "spiritual" and what really mattered was "how you lived your life."

A classmate, Christy, appearing to sympathize with Bob's

viewpoint, offered that questions appeared to exist about the accuracy of what the New Testament says about Jesus. She made reference to the "gospels" that had been excluded from the Bible, including the Gospel of Thomas. Unable to resist (I had studied these issues), I interjected that historians have shown that those other gospels were written considerably later than the canonical gospels to which Christy readily agreed. I then asked them both if they thought Christ existed. Was he a real person? While Bob wasn't sure anymore, Christy, a professional historian, acknowledged that he probably or certainly did exist.

I repeated what I had learned in my study, that very few historians question the historicity of Jesus. Then I offered C.S. Lewis's quip that if Christ did exist he was either a liar, a lunatic or Lord, asking Bob if he thought someone who was a liar or a lunatic would be a great person or role model.

The conversation unfortunately ended prematurely, but we had become engaged in the very type of "courageous conversation" that LMR sought to encourage, and we all said we'd get back together another time to pursue the questions.

As I walked out, I thought to myself with a wry grin, that I might have just had my first apologetic moment. Christy joined me as we headed for our matching Volvos, coincidentally parked very near each other. She commented that I seemed to have a keen interest in the questions of faith that we had begun to touch on. I don't know why I did this, but I replied rather glibly, "Yes, I do, but it's a really long story. You'll have to read the book." She appeared understandably confused by my statement, so I briefly explained the journey I had been on.

She responded by asking, "So how has all that turned out for you?"

For an instant I panicked. *What was my answer?* I urgently thought. Then I quickly responded, "I've recommitted myself to Christ."

She said simply, "That's great," and we said goodnight.

But had I? Had I honestly recommitted myself to Christ? I was still searching for answers. I was still reading books and listening to podcasts. I may have accepted Christ intellectually but not emotionally—not volitionally. This realization reminded me of something Alistair Begg said, that becoming a Christian requires decisive action. It's not "just a decision that's been made along the journey."

In one of his sermons, Begg stressed that making a genuine commitment to Jesus is life changing. Accepting Christ, he went on, is *not* like saying, "I've been very lax when it comes to exercise, and I've decided to join a club and do some running around because it would be good for me, and it's a good example for my children. All of that is fine," he continued, "but that is *not* what the Bible is describing in becoming a Christian."[56] I wondered if I had, in Begg's words, just "made a decision along the way." Was I like the Tom Hanks character in *Angels and Demons* who had "not yet received the gift of faith"?

Despite these questions, I had become more and more confident about the weight of evidence supporting the conclusion that the story and the reality of Jesus were correct. So much so, that I wondered what I needed to accept "on faith." I had gone from having an expectation that belief would require an enormous, irrational leap to wondering if the reality of Christ was so reasonable, so supported by evidence, I might not need to accept anything merely by faith.

Since the Bible and numerous commentators often spoke about "faith," I again posed a question for myself: What do Christians believe as a result of faith, and what do they believe because of their experience?

I wrote down what I thought was the clearest statement of faith in the Bible, Hebrews 11:1: "Now, faith is being sure of what we hope for and certain of what we do not see." If this is the test, what was it that "we hope for" and what is it that "we do not see"? As I was struggling with this issue, I listened to an interview on the Apologetics 315 website[57] during which the guest mentioned that the word *faith* had lost its meaning in contemporary society and that *confident trust* is a good substitute for the word *faith*. That reference reminded me of a message by Alistair Begg entitled "What is Faith?"[58]

I found that podcast still in my iTunes library, and during my next morning run, I listened to it again. Probably the reason I made the connection was that Begg said something similar about faith. Central to faith, he said, is trust in what Christ has done. He said, "Faith is knowledge, assent to the knowledge, and trust on the basis of the knowledge to which I've given assent." He continued, "Knowledge and assent are less than trust." Begg then used the analogy of a title deed. Christians have been given a title deed to heaven that they have not seen. Just as we trust that property represented by a deed is real even if we haven't seen it, we need to trust that heaven and all the promises of Christ are real even if we have not seen them.[59]

Begg finally posed this question, "How do you come to faith in Jesus Christ?" Answering his own questions, Begg offered:

> *Stage 1—knowledge; who is this Jesus? What did he do? When did He come? When did He live? Is He alive? See, it involves your mind, it involves thinking. Some of us haven't come to faith because we don't think. We want an experience to come down and grab us and whisk us off our feet and take us somewhere.*[60]

Begg then went on to clarify that "intellectual assent cannot be equated with genuine faith," and, moreover, many fail to come to faith because even with knowledge and assent, their "assent has never given way to personal trust in what Christ has done on the cross."[61]

For months I had been very close to ending the journey and admitting that somewhere along the way I had already made up my mind. Yet, I was still listening to Begg, Keller, and Zacharias three or four times a week during morning runs. Typically I ran forty-five or fifty minutes, about the length of two podcasts. But sometimes the message would end before I completed my run and the iPod played whatever the next track was on the playlist.

Although I regularly changed the podcasts I would be listening to and set them first on the playlist, I had a list of miscellaneous songs that would play next, and that list was often unchanged for a few weeks. So, after listening to a Begg, Zacharias, or Keller podcast message, often a song would start playing next. Because I had not changed the list for some time, I noticed the same song began to play—a love song by Colbie Caillat. This particular morning though, I couldn't ignore the lyrics or the timing of hearing, "I don't know but I think I may be fallin' for you."[62] I was preoccupied thinking about God and it did seem as if I had been "waiting all my life and now I found you." And, like the words of the refrain, I was afraid of admitting my attraction (afraid of what commitment might mean) and, therefore, like the singer, it seemed as if I wanted to keep my interest "to myself."

While it may sound trite, the song put everything into focus. As I listened to the words, the song caused me to think about where I was on my journey. Wasn't it the case that I'd been spending a lot of time thinking about God? Wasn't it the case that I thought I was "falling for" Christ? And wasn't it the case that I waited all my life for such a relationship?

The last time this song came on during a run after a podcast, a new thought occurred to me. Despite the triteness of the lyrics, wasn't a relationship with God really like a love affair?

This thought led me to realize that during this process I constantly noted how extraordinary my wife is. The way she lived was the way I thought everyone should—including me. She had always been incredibly patient with me over so many things. And most of all, I realized how much more I loved her every day. Cheryl had been Christlike in her way of life, her patience, and her love for me. And if Christianity is true, Christ had done even more for me. Hadn't he waited very patiently for me? Hadn't he forgiven me of my self-centeredness, my arrogant individualism, and various other sins? And if it was all true, hadn't he even died for me?

In my dating years, I was terribly afraid of rejection, so I often delayed asking someone out until I had figured out that she would almost certainly say yes. With a relationship with Jesus, I already knew that he says, "Yes." In fact, as observed earlier, was he not "the Hound of Heaven" on my trail? He was actually pursuing me! And here was a relationship that would endure. The fog was lifting, and clarity was setting in. Clearly I had no need to ignore reason and take the proverbial leap of faith.

Once I concluded with a high degree of comfort and conviction that not only did Christ exist but that he was the Son of God, I wondered what I should do and how my life might change. I continued to resist answering those questions and accepting what was in front of me. I wondered if we all aren't like Thomas, seeking just a little more proof, asking to touch and feel the resurrected Christ before believing. I didn't need more proof, but I did fear the responsibility that would accompany a renewed commitment to Christ. I knew that commitment meant I would have to walk away from the other things in which I placed my trust, the three big "Ps"—things like my professional influence (power), my acquisition of wealth (profits), and my desire for personal recognition (profile).

I had always trusted myself, so changing my allegiance would be difficult. I sought the praise of other people rather than the praise of God—something Jesus said was an obstacle to faith (John 5:44). Thus, I could now see a "leap of faith" was actually necessary—but as I now understood, it was a "leap of *trust*."

Ravi Zacharias had said something a year earlier that seemed to fit, if not explain, my situation. "Is it possible," he asked, "that God has put just enough information and evidence of him in the world to attract our attention, but he also left out just enough so that the actual commitment to him requires enough focus and commitment that once the leap is made it is sincere and abiding?"[63] Remarkably, much of the wisdom I had received on my many early morning runs was coming back to me in profound ways. I wondered, but did not dwell on, why I took so long, why I had persistently suppressed the evidence before me.

I recognized that I probably had exhausted the issues and the analysis. At this point, I was "kicking against the goads" (Acts 26:14, ASV). I could keep reading and listening, but what I really needed was trust. And if Christ had been resurrected, which I believed he had, I really had no other choice but to trust him. In Alistair Begg's language, I had had the knowledge for a long time, and I had assented to that knowledge. Now I had to trust.

But I wasn't comfortable trusting anyone but myself. That had been my credo for fifty years, and by some measures it had served me well. My reluctance to commit—truly commit—was born out of fear. I was afraid to trust anything or anybody other than myself. I also feared the obligations that would likely flow from such a commitment.

Yet, I *knew* Christianity was true. I *knew* it was right. I *knew* it was something I wanted. I *knew* it was something I needed. Huck Finn's words of frustration at the end of Mark Twain's famous book came to mind. "All right then," Huck says, "I'll go to hell." I said something similar, "All right, then, I give in. I surrender."

Begg suggested that if a person is prepared to move from knowledge to assent to trust, "You can tell him that you do know you are a sinner, you do understand Christ to be the savior you just acknowledged you need, that you do recognize that faith is action, it is life changing—you will never be the same again—but that you do want to be laid hold of by his embrace, gathered up, caught into him, as it were, so that you might be not simply an observer in the hall of faith, but that however small your portrait, however short the years on the name plate, that your name might appear there." And that's what I did.

At the end of his book, *The Reason for God*, Tim Keller offers the following prayer for any of the readers who might then be persuaded to make a personal commitment to God:

> *Father, I've always believed in you and Jesus Christ, but my heart's fundamental trust was elsewhere—in my own competence and decency. This has only gotten me into trouble. As far as I know my own heart, today I give it to you, I transfer my trust to you, and ask*

*that you would receive and accept me not for anything I have done
but because of everything Christ has done for me.*[64]

I offered that prayer as well. Although I still have many
questions—that's what lawyers do best—I made a commitment to
put this renewed faith into action, "a sustained attitude." Perhaps
more than anything I realized C.S. Lewis was right when he said
of Christianity that the "only thing it could not be is of moderate
importance."

During this journey I also read the Bible through in a year.
During that process, I ran across various passages and stories that
bothered me and raised questions, some of which were particularly
troublesome. For example, I wasn't sure how a forgiving God could
encourage the annihilation of the Canaanites when the Israelites
moved into the Promised Land. And I still didn't know to what
extent I, as a Christian, should eschew worldly goods. While I
have many questions I still want to pursue, however, I am often
reminded of Alistair Begg's advice to keep focused on the "main
things" and to keep "the main things plain." If I believe that Christ
lived and died for me, everything else is different—that's the
"main thing." Thus, even if I don't understand the gift of tongues
or presuppositional apologetics, I need to stay focused on Christ
crucified. I can prayerfully consider those "secondary" questions,
but I shouldn't lose sight of the *main thing*, to live my life so that
in the long run I might be able to say, "I have fought the good
fight. I have finished the race. I have kept the faith." So, for me,
I'm going to keep running.

EPILOGUE
(RUNNING WITH RAVI)

The obsession with running is really an
obsession for more and more life.

—George Sheehan

I believe in Christianity as I believe the sun has risen, not only
because I see it, but because by it I see everything else.

—C.S. Lewis

I have come that they may have life, and that
they may have it more abundantly.

—John 10:10 (KJV)

It was four years, almost to the day, since I had shown up for my first, one-mile group run with the YMCA 10K Training Team. I was back on the same piece of grass in front of the Oates Theater at Collegiate School, but this time I was an assistant coach for novice runners. Standing nearby, Cheryl was in her second year as a coach for walkers. I had come a long way.

Two months later, I started teaching a class in "Christian Apologetics" at Christ Lutheran. As I prepared for those first sessions I reflected on the arguments I had studied and how I was now getting ready to teach them. I was trying to recall how I had first responded to the cosmological and teleological arguments when a curious thought occurred to me—having become convinced that Christianity is true by whatever evidence, proofs, arguments, or collections of arguments led me to that conclusion, the support for my convictions do not rest on my favorite "arguments"—I now recognized that such "arguments" may be signposts to or clues of God, but they don't sustain belief. Rather, as the suppression of the truth is lifted and doubt is assuaged, each of the arguments and all of the evidence of God becomes not only clear, but each builds on the next in such a way that the conclusion becomes both powerful and compelling, if not self-evident. I recite the creeds with conviction and confidence.

By the end of the journey, my thinking about God and Jesus was no longer limited to Sunday mornings or to an intellectual investigation. Rather than compartmentalizing my thoughts or working through various "arguments," I now understand my "worldview"—those fundamental beliefs that affect my thinking and doing every day. I find that, as C.S. Lewis said so eloquently: "I believe in Christianity as I believe the sun has risen, not only because I see it, but because by it I see everything else."

Just as I was completing this manuscript, I travelled to Norcross, Georgia to meet Ravi Zacharias and Stuart McAllister. If the reconciliation of my physical and spiritual health was not in itself a miracle, their invitation for me to train to become a member of one of their teams speaking on apologetics can be explained only in terms of God's providence. Whoever would have thought? I am, however, looking forward to running with them and seeing where God takes me.

Bruce's Race Times				
DATE	**EVENT**	**TIME**		
		YEAR 1	**YEAR 2**	**YEAR 3**
January	Frostbite 15K			1:35:47
February	Colonial ½ (Williamsburg)		2:30:01	
April	Monument Avenue 10K	1:04:20	58:42	55:10
April	Boston Marathon			4:59:13
April	Charlottesville Marathon		5:30:40	
May	Race for Cure 5K	30:00		
May	James River Scramble 10K	?		1:15:24
May	Carytown 10K	1:03:15	56:30	59:54
May	Edinburgh Marathon		4:59:22	
August	Patrick Henry ½ Marathon			2:40:18
September	Va. Beach ½ Marathon	2:13:59	2:40:14	2:24:46
September	McDonald's ½ (Maymont)	2:10:30		
October	Capital 10 Miler			1:40:58
October	Scholarship 30K	3:40:09		
November	ING NYC Marathon	4:57:28		5:09:38
November	Richmond Marathon	5:11:45	5:21:59	
November	Richmond ½ Marathon			2:13:51
November	Turkey Trot 10K (U of R)	?	1:05:39	1:04

Eleven Commandments of Running

1. Find your pace.

2. Listen to your body.

3. Enter many local races.

4. Get a running buddy.

5. Shop at your local running store.

6. Join your local running club.

7. Watch *Chariots of Fire* at least once.

8. Join a training team or running group.

9. Volunteer for some local races.

10. Enjoy the time on your feet.

11. Whatever distance it is, go for a long run.

Top Ten Arguments for the Existence of the God of the Bible

1. Resurrection of Christ
   (How do we explain the blood of the martyrs?)

2. Moral code within [axiological argument]
   (What is the source of right and wrong?)

3. Consciousness and the uniqueness of human beings
   (Why are we self-aware? Why are we materially different
   from other species?)

4. The historicity of Jesus
   (Is there any doubt that Christ lived and died?)

5. Lives of great Christians—The durability of Christianity
   (What explains the faith of believers?)

6. Presence of intelligent design [teleological argument]
   (What explains the complexity of and the intelligence we
   find in life?)

7. Rightness of Christian values ("Let your light so shine . . .")
   (Why do we value humility, generosity, and grace over
   pride, greed, and selfishness?)

8. The finely tuned world [anthropic argument]
   (Why does it appear that the universe was created
   for us?)

9. Starry skies above [cosmological argument]
   (Why is there something rather than nothing?)

10. Desire for God
    (Why do we have a sense for and seek the transcendent?)

BIBLIOGRAPHY

A considerable amount of study, analysis, and information was gathered from listening to podcasts or sermon downloads from RZIM (Ravi Zacharias), Truth for Life (Alistair Begg), and Redeemer Presbyterian (Timothy Keller) as well as a few others. The books I read (or listened to) include the following:

Berlinski, David. *The Devil's Delusion: Atheism and its Scientific Pretensions*. New York: Basic Books 2009.

Boa, Ken & Larry Moody. *I'm Glad You Asked*. Wheaton, IL: Victor Books 1994.

Buckley, William. *God and Man at Yale*. Washington, DC: Regnery 1951.

Burpo, Todd & Lynn Vincent. *Heaven Is for Real: A Little Boy's Astounding Story of His Trip to Heaven and Back* Nashville: Thomas Nelson, 2010.

Copan, Paul. *Is God a Moral Monster?* Grand Rapids, MI: Baker Books, 2011.

Collins, Francis S. *The Language of God: A Scientist Presents Evidence for Belief.* New York: Free Press 2006.

Colson, Charles & Nancy Pearcey. *How Now Shall We Live?* Wheaton, IL: Tyndale House Publishers, 1999.

Colson, Charles. *Loving God*. Grand Rapids, MI: Zondervan, 1996.

D'Souza, Dinesh. *What's So Great About Christianity?* Washington, DC: Regnery Press, 2007.

Dawkins, Richard. *The God Delusion*. New York: Houghton Mifflin, 2006.

Ebel, C. Thomas. *Walk Ten Steps with the Lord*. Maitland, FL: Xulon Press, 2011.

Ehrman, Bart D. *Misquoting Jesus*. San Francisco: HarperSanFrancisco, 2005.

Galloway, Jeff. *Marathon—You Can Do It!* Bolinas, CA: Shelter Publications, 2001.

Geisler, Norman L. *Christian Apologetics*. Spokane, WA: Prince Press, 2003.

Geisler, Norman & Frank Turek. *I Don't Have Enough Faith to be an Atheist*. Wheaton, IL: Crossway, 2004.

Gladwell, Malcolm. *Blink: The Power of Thinking Without Thinking*. New York: Little Brown & Co. , 2005.

Gladwell, Malcolm. *Outliers: The Story of Success*. New York: Little Brown & Co. , 2008.

Gladwell, Malcolm. *The Tipping Point: How Little Things Can Make a Big Difference*. New York: Little Brown & Co. , 2000.

Gladwell, Malcolm. *What the Dog Saw: And Other Adventures*. New York: Little Brown & Co. , 2009.

Goldstein, Rebecca Newberger. *36 Arguments for the Existence of God*. New York: Vintage, 2011.

Gray, John. *Straw Dogs*. London: Granta Books, 2002.

Guinness, Os. *Long Journey Home*. Colorado Springs: Waterbrook Press, 2001.

Harris, Sam. *The End of Faith: Religion, Terror and the Future of Reason*. New York: W. W. Norton, 2004.

Harris, Sam. *Letter to a Christian Nation*. New York: Vintage, 2008.

Harris, Sam. *The Moral Landscape*. New York: Free Press, 2010.

Horton, David, ed. *The Portable Seminary*. Minneapolis: Bethany House, 2006.

Karnazes, Dean. *Ultramarathon Man*. New York: Penguin Books, 2005.

Keller, Timothy. *Counterfeit Gods: The Empty Promises of Money, Sex, and the Only Hope that Matters*. Hialeah, FL: Dutton Press, 2009.

Keller, Timothy. *The Reason for God: Belief in an Age of Skepticism*. Hialeah, FL: Dutton Press, 2008.

Keller, Timothy. *The Prodigal God: Recovering the Heart of the Christian Faith*. Hialeah, FL: Dutton Press, 2008.

Lennox, John C. *God's Undertaker: Has Science Buried God?* London: Lion Hudson, 2009.

Lennox, John C. *Gunning for God: Why the New Atheists are Missing the Target*. London: Lion Hudson, 2011.

Lennox, John C. *Seven Days that Divide the World*. Grand Rapids: Zondervan, 2011.

Lewis, C. S. *Mere Christianity*. New York: Touchstone, 1996.

Lewis, C. S. *Surprised By Joy*. New York: Houghton Mifflin Harcourt, 1995.

Liddell, Eric. *The Disciplines of the Christian Life*. Escondido, CA: eChristian Books, 2012.

Lindsley, Art. *True Truth*. Downers Grove, IL: InterVarsity Press, 2004.

Lindsley, Art. *C. S. Lewis's Case for Christ*. Downers Grove, IL: InterVarsity Press, 2005.

McDougall, Christopher. *Born to Run: A Hidden Tribe, Superathletes, and the Greatest Race the World Has Never Seen*. New York: Vintage, 2009.

McGrath, Alister. *The Twilight of Atheism*. New York: Doubleday, 2004.

McGrath, Alister and Joanna C. McGrath. *The Dawkins Delusion: Atheist Fundamentalism and the Denial of the Divine*. Lancaster, PA: Veritas Books, 2010.

Metaxas, Eric. *Bonhoffer: Pastor, Martyr, Prophet, Spy: A Righteous Gentile Against the Third Reich*. Blackstone Audio, 2010)

Eric Metaxas, *Amazing Grace: William Wilberforce and the Heroic Campaign to End Slavery.* Newark, NJ: Audible Audio, 2007.

Niesluchowski, Dana & Dave Veerman. *The Runner's Devotional.* Wheaton, IL: Tyndale House, 2011.

Pierce, William J. , M. Scott Murr, & Raymond F. Moss, *Run Less Run Faster.* Emmaus, PA: Rodale, 2007.

Piper, Don. *90 Minutes in Heaven.* Grand Rapids, MI: Revell, 2004.

Rice, Anne. *Called Out of Darkness.* New York: Knopf, 2008.

Schaeffer, Francis A. *He Is There and He Is Not Silent.* Wheaton, IL: Tyndale House, 1972.

Sire, James W. *The Universe Next Door.* Downers Grove, IL: InterVarsity Press, 2009.

Strobel, Lee. *The Case for Christ: A Journalist's Personal Investigation of the Evidence for Jesus.* Grand Rapids, MI: Zondervan, 1998.

Strobel, Lee. *The Case for Faith: A Journalist Investigates the Toughest Objections to Christianity.* Grand Rapids, MI: Zondervan, 2000.

Strobel, Lee. *The Case for the Real Jesus: A Journalist Investigates Current Attacks on the Identity of Christ.* Grand Rapids, MI: Zondervan, 2007.

Ramsey, Russell W. *God's Joyful Runner.* Getzville, NY: Bridge Publishing, 1987.

Stark, Rodney. *The Rise of Christianity: How the Obscure, Marginal Jesus Movement Became the Dominant Religious Force in the Western World in a Few Centuries.* San Francisco: HarperOne, 1996.

Stearns, Richard. *The Hole in Our Gospel.* Nashville: Thomas Nelson, 2009.

Vanauken, Sheldon. *A Severe Mercy.* San Francisco: HarperCollins, 1977.

Wolpe, David J. *Why Faith Matters.* San Francisco: HarperOne, 2008.

Wright, N. T. *Simply Christian: Why Christianity Makes Sense.* San Francisco: HarperOne, 2006.

Yasso, Bart. *My Life on the Run: The Wit, Wisdom, and Insights of a Road Racing Icon.* Emmaus, PA: Rodale, 2008.

Zacharias, Ravi. *Can Man Live Without God?* Nashville: W Publishing, 1994.

Zacharias, Ravi, ed. *Beyond Opinion: Living the Faith We Defend.* Nashville: Thomas Nelson, 2007.

Zacharias, Ravi. *End of Faith.* Grand Rapids, MI: Zondervan, 2008.

Zacharias, Ravi. *Grand Weaver.* Grand Rapids, MI: Zondervan, 2007.

Zacharias, Ravi. *Walking East to West.* Grand Rapids, MI: Zondervan, 2009.

Zacharias, Ravi. *Why Jesus?* New York: FaithWords, 2011.

Zacharias Ravi & Norman Giesler. *Who Made God?* Grand Rapids, MI: Zondervan, 2003.

Also I listened to the following tape or CD series/courses: From The Teaching company and/or the C.S. Lewis Institute:

- *Basic Apologetics Courses* (Dr. Art Lindsley)
- *Philosophy of Religion* (Professor James Hall, 2003)
- *Lives of Great Christians* (Professor William R. Cook, 2007)
- *The Historical Jesus* (Professor Bart D. Ehrman, 2000)
- *Books that Have Made History: Books that Can Change Your Life* (Professor J. Rufus Fears, 2005)
- *Life and Writings of C.S. Lewis* (Professor Louis Markos)
- *Questions of Value* (Professor Patrick Grim, 2005)
- *Utopia and Terror in the 20th Century* (Professor Vejas Gabriel Liulevicius, 2003)
- *The History of Christianity in the Reformation Era* (Professor Brad S. Gregory, 2001)
- *The Great Ideas of Philosophy, 2nd Edition* (Professor Daniel N. Robinson, 2004)

ENDNOTES

[1] *Apostles' Creed.* http://www.elca.org/What-We-Believe/Statements-of-Belief/The-Apostles-Creed.aspx (last accessed on January 15, 2011).

[2] C. S. Lewis, "Christian Apologetics" from *God in the Dock* (Grand Rapids, MI: Wm. B. Eerdmans Publishing, 1970; reprinted 2001), 101; also in Lesley Walmsley, ed., *C.S. Lewis Essay Collection: Faith, Christianity and the Church* (London: HarperCollins, 2000).

[3] Carl Sagan, *Cosmos* (New York: Ballantine 1993), 4.

[4] Dr. Benjamin Wiker, "Exclusive Flew" interview tothesource.org, 30 October 2007. See also Anthony Flew and Roy Abraham Varghese, *There Is a God: How the World's Most Notorious Atheist Changed His Mind,* San Francisco: HarperOne, 2007.

[5] Norman Geisler and Frank Turek, *I Don't Have Enough Faith to Be an Atheist* (Wheaton, IL: Crossway, 2004), 106.

[6] Freeman Dyson, *Disturbing the Universe* (New York: Harper & Row, 1979), 250.

[7] Fred Hoyle, "The Universe: Past and Present Reflections." *Engineering and Science,* November 1981, 8–12.

[8] Hugh Ross, *The Creator and the Cosmos, third edition* (Colorado Springs: NavPress, 2001). This quotation even spawned a book about these questions of creationism and Darwinism. See James Perloff, *Tornado in a Junkyard: The Relentless Myth of Darwinism* (Arlington, MA: Refuge, 1999). (The original analogy was drawn by astronomer Fred Hoyle in 1981, as quoted in "Hoyle on Evolution," *Nature,* Vol. 294, 12 November 1981, 105.)

[9] Francis Collins, *The Language of God: A Scientist Presents Evidence for Belief* (New York: Free Press, 2006), 187–95. For Collins, intelligent design is a "God of the gaps" and he believes that science will fill those gaps eventually. Hence, Collins embraces "theistic evolution"—an approach that synthesizes science and faith by explaining evolution as a vehicle in God's master plan. Finally, he devotes a chapter in his book making the case for the adoption of a new term—"BioLogos"—for the harmony he sees by maintaining faith in science as well as God, Ibid., 203. See www.biologos.org/.

[10] Ibid., 75. These observations also find themselves often as part of an argument to God based upon "statistical probability." J. Warner Wallace's apologetics website, "Please Convince Me"—www.pleaseconvinceme.com—has a good article about the "argument from statistical improbability."

[11] Ibid., 78. Collins also restates quotations from the famous physicist Stephen Hawking, who wrote: "The odds against a universe like ours emerging out of something like the Big Bang are enormous. I think there are clearly

religious implications." Moreover, he cites Hawking as also saying, "it would be very difficult to explain why the universe would have begun in just this way except as the act of a God who intended to create beings like us." Hawking appears to have abandoned these observations with the 2010 publication of his book (written with Leonard Mlodinow), *The Grand Design* (New York: Bantam, 2010).

[12] Bart Yasso, *My Life on the Run* (New York: Rodale, 2008), 260.

[13] Official Program, Bank of America Chicago Marathon (2010), 92–93.

[14] http://www.cbcf.org/en-US/About%20CBCF/Media%20Centre/News%20 Releases/2010%20Run%20Day.aspx.

[15] *Running USA*, August 11, 2010 (http://www.runningusa.org/).

[16] *Runner's World* (September 19, 1996) (http://www.runnersworld.com/).

[17] Post-modernism: "A postmodern perspective is skeptical of any grounded theoretical perspectives. It rejects the certainties of modernism and approaches art, science, literature, and philosophy with a pessimistic, disillusioned outlook. Questioning the possibility of clear meaning or truth, this worldview is about discontinuity, suspicion of motive, and an acceptance of logical incoherence." Amy Orr-Ewing, "Postmodern Challenges to the Bible," *Beyond Opinion*. Ravi Zacharias, ed. (Nashville: Thomas Nelson, 2007), 3.

[18] Author's notes from listening to J. Rufus Fears, "Books that Have Made History: Books that Can Change Your Life" (Chantilly, VA: The Teaching Company, n.d.).

[19] Arthur Leff, "Unspeakable Ethics Unnatural Law," *Duke LJ* (Durham, NC: Duke University, 1979), 1229.

[20] Ibid., 1240.

[21] Ibid., 1241. ("At some point in every sustained argument about what is right or wrong, or what ought or ought not to be done, some normative proposition about who has the final power over normative propositions will have to be asserted.").

[22] N. T. Wright, *Simply Christian* (San Francisco, HarperOne, 2006).

[23] Bart D. Ehrman, *Misquoting Jesus* (New York: HarperCollins, 2005).

[24] Bertrand Russell, *Why I Am Not a Christian and Other Essays on Religion and Related Subject* (New York: Touchstone Books, 1967), 16.

[25] Gleason Archer, "The Witness of the Bible to Its Own Inerrancy" as reproduced in *The Foundation of Biblical Authority*, James M. Boice, ed. (London: Pickering & Inglis, 1979), 86–87; http://www.biblicalstudies. org.uk/article_witness_archer.html.

[26] Josh McDowell, *The New Evidence that Demands a Verdict* (Nashville: Thomas Nelson, 1999), 120.

[27] Ibid.

[28] C. S. Lewis, *Mere Christianity* (New York: Touchstone Books, 1996), 56.

[29] Charles Colson, "The Paradox of Power" (www.powertochange.com).

[30] Tertullian, *The Apology*, chapter L as cited in *Latin Christianity: Its Founder, Tetullian* (originally published in 1885 as the 10-volume collection titled *Anti-Necene Fathers*) found at http://www.ccel.org/ccel/schaff/anf03.iv.iii .l.html?highlight=seed#highlight (last accessed on December 30, 2010) (emphasis added).

[31] Francis Thompson, "The Hound of Heaven" in *The Hound of Heaven* (New York: Dodd, Mead, and Co. , 1922).

[32] Ravi Zacharias, *Can Man Live Without God?* (Nashville: Thomas Nelson, 1994), 183.

[33] Malcolm Gladwell, *Blink: The Power of Thinking without Thinking* (New York: Little, Brown & Co. , 2007).

[34] *Mere Christianity,* 30.

[35] C. S. Lewis, "Is Theology Poetry?" *Weight of Glory and Other Addresses* (New York: HarperCollins, 1949, 1980), 140.

[36] Rodney Stark, *The Rise of Christianity: How the Obscure, Marginal Jesus Movement Became the Dominant Religious Force in the Western World in a Few Centuries* (San Francisco: HarperOne, 1996), 84. ("Pagan and Christian writers are unanimous not only that Christian Scripture stressed love and charity as the central duties of faith, but that these were sustained in everyday behavior," 86). Stark also explains that these notions of charity, kindness, care giving, and love for strangers (non-Christians), especially in the face of danger to themselves were utterly new ideas at the time of the early years of the new Christian church. Ibid.

[37] Richard Dawkins, *The God Delusion* (New York: Houghton Mifflin Harcourt, 2006).

[38] Ibid., 5.

[39] Ibid., 221.

[40] Ibid., 216.

[41] Ibid., 218.

[42] Ibid., 216.

[43] http://www.merriam-webster.com/dictionary/altruism.

[44] http://www.britannica.com/EBchecked/topic/17855/altruism.

[45] Richard Dawkins, *The Greatest Show on Earth* (New York: Free Press, 2009).

[46] *God Delusion,* 220–21.

[47] Ibid., 212–13.

[48] Ibid., 227.

[49] Ibid., 228.

[50] Ibid.

[51] Ibid., 229.

[52] Ibid.

[53] Ibid., 229.

[54] Ibid.

[55] Ibid., 5.

[56] Alistair Begg, "Go and Tell Them" (podcast, May 8, 2010), http://www.truthforlife.org.

[57] www.apologetics315.com.

[58] Alistair Begg, "What is Faith?" (podcast, November 15–16, 2007), http://www.truthforlife.org.

[59] Ibid.

[60] Ibid.

[61] Ibid.

[62] Colbie Caillet & Rick Nowels, "Fallin' For You."

[63] Ravi Zacharias, *The End of Reason* (Grand Rapids, MI: Zondervan, 2008), 75.

[64] Timothy Keller, *The Reason for God* (New York: Penguin Group, 2008), 235.